# NARCISSIST

# THEODORE O'MALSOMIGHI

# Copyright 2019 by Theodore O'Malsomighi

## All rights reserved.

This document is geared towards providing exact and reliable information with regards to the topic and issue covered. The publication is sold with the idea that the publisher is not required to render accounting, officially permitted, or otherwise, qualified services. If advice is necessary, legal or professional, a practiced individual in the profession should be ordered.

From a Declaration of Principles which was accepted and approved equally by a Committee of the American Bar Association and a Committee of Publishers and Associations.

In no way is it legal to reproduce, duplicate, or transmit any part of this document in either electronic means or in printed format. Recording of this publication is strictly prohibited and any storage of this document is not allowed unless with written permission from the publisher. All rights reserved.

The information provided herein is stated to be truthful and consistent, in that any liability, in terms of inattention or otherwise, by any usage or abuse of any policies, processes, or directions contained within is

# Table of Contents

# Book Description

Do you know someone who is overly arrogant, shows an extreme lack of empathy, or exhibits an inflated sense of entitlement? Do they exploit others, or engage in magical thinking? These are all traits of narcissistic personality disorder, and when it comes to dealing with narcissists, it can be difficult to get your point across. So how do you handle the narcissistic people in your life? You might interact with them in social or professional settings, and you might even love one—so ignoring them isn't really a practical solution. They're frustrating, and maybe even intimidating, but ultimately, you need to find a way of communicating effectively with them.

By learning to anticipate and avoid certain hot-button issues, you'll be able to relate to narcissists without triggering aggression. By validating some common narcissistic concerns, you'll also find out how to be heard in conversation with a narcissist.

This book will help you learn to meet your own needs while side-stepping unproductive power struggles and senseless arguments with someone who is at the center of his or her own universe. This new edition also includes new chapters on dealing with narcissistic women, aggressive and abusive narcissists, strategies for safety, and the link between narcissism and sex addiction.

Everybody needs some healthy narcissism. But in a society obsessed with appearance, wealth, and status, it's easy for problematic narcissists to thrive. Many people who seem to "have it all" are suffering from one of the most common-and overlooked-personality disorders today: high level narcissism. Typified by an obsession with perfection, a desperate need for admiration, and a willingness to use and exploit others for personal gain, high level narcissism can spell devastation for anyone who crosses the narcissist's path.

In Freeing Yourself from the Narcissist in Your Life, psychotherapist Linda Martinez-Lewi presents an in-depth and supportive plan for identifying, understanding, and dealing with high level narcissistic behavior in those close to you. Martinez-Lewi helps you to liberate yourself from draining personal relationships with narcissists, and shows how to regain a sense of peace, balance, and well-being.

Finally, you'll learn how to set limits with your narcissist and when it's time to draw the line on unacceptable behavior.

# INTRODUCTION

There is a silent epidemic happening right under our noses: the epidemic of narcissistic abuse. People are experiencing it in their homes and in the workplace. They may not understand what is happening. They may feel they are going crazy. Even if they could prove the abuse they are suffering, they fear they will not be believed, and their lives are being ruined. By learning to recognize narcissistic abuse, we can stop it from happening to ourselves, our loved ones and our co-workers.

Narcissists look like everyone else. They may be good looking and may seem charming, glib and friendly. They are not. Beneath their false exterior, a monster is waiting. Narcissists are childish, manipulative and cruel. They believe they are entitled to whatever they want, whether they have earned it or not - and they will do whatever it takes to get it. If they don't get it, they will react with rage or cold, silent hatred. They will spread lies about you to your family, friends, coworkers, even your children. They will tell people you are crazy, that you are abusive, that you are manipulative, that you are a liar, that you are sexually promiscuous, anything to destroy your reputation. They will try to get you fired, arrested, ostracized and disowned. The purpose of these narcissistic lies is literally to destroy you and anything good that you have.

Anyone can become the target of a narcissist if they possess things the narcissist envies. This could be material things, talents, friends, a family... Narcissists cannot stand to see other people happy and will work hard to ruin it, even if the person they are ruining is their parent, child, sibling, friend or spouse. They will use projection and other crazy -making behaviors to cloud the truth to the point that the victim can no longer even remember what it is.

If a loved one or co-worker constantly blames you for things that are in no way your fault, if they deny guilt even when caught red-handed, if they change their stance or opinion on something just to oppose yours (even when you are trying to agree with them), if you are constantly off-balance because one day something is OK but the next day it isn't - to the point that you can never do anything right, if they are constantly accusing you of saying, feeling and doing things that you don't, if you feel like nothing is ever good enough for them, if they lie about you to other people, if they expect you to set yourself on fire just to keep them warm... you are dealing with a narcissist.

Once you understand that, things can change. There is help. You can learn from this very book what to do to stop it. There are millions suffering in silence because they don't know what they are dealing with or how to get out of it. So many victims of horrible abuse are being that told the problem is them. What narcissists fear most is being exposed for the abusers and liars they really are. They depend on the fact that their abuse is so outrageous, people will not believe the victim. Shine a light on their darkness and share the knowledge with everyone you know. Spread the awareness. Stop the smear campaign.

# What is a Narcissist?

What's a narcissist? Do you think you know any right now? The word narcissist is used so often, it's meaning has become a bit watered down. Remember that Elliot Rodger kid and his manifesto? That's a narcissist. He is an excellent example of Narcissistic Personality Disorder, and how destructive and dangerous it is.

The common image most people have of what a narcissist is, is generally not correct. Most people envision an arrogant, suave man or a selfish, image-obsessed woman. These things are sometimes related to narcissism, but they are not even close to the whole picture. The true narcissist is not just vain and arrogant. They are so much worse than that. Narcissists will go to whatever lengths they have to in order to get what they want and so often - as we see with Elliot Rodger - what they want is revenge. They are angry, childish, vengeful and dangerous personalities who want to punish others. They believe they have been wronged and they react with rage when the world does not give them what they want. They take pleasure in hurting people, especially those who care about them. The goal of the narcissist is literally to destroy, especially someone they think cares about them. It is very fortunate this person never found a girlfriend; he probably wouldn't have killed her so long as she did not leave him but her entire existence would have been absolutely miserable. Abuse is integral in the "relationship" with a narcissist. It is all they know and the only way they can feel better. The narcissist cares not at all for their partner as a person; the partner only matters inasmuch as what they can do for the narcissist. It is very hard for normal, caring people to understand this and because of that, they often hang on to the relationship thinking they can reach the narcissist. They cannot. A narcissist cannot be reached with love and you cannot appeal to his good graces. He is capable of neither.

The narcissist is like a shark, or a machine that is designed to do only one thing. He cannot be swayed, appealed to, reasoned with, deviated or stopped. Hurting you literally makes him feel better. That's the way it is. You can never make him feel good enough that he will stop. Never. You cannot change him, fix him or "love" him out of it. The only thing you can do is get out of the way. These people are fundamentally broken and as soon as the narcissist decides that you can no longer provide him with the sustenance he needs, he will drop you without a second glance. It could take 2 months, it could take 10 years, it could take 3 days but after he has sucked you dry, he will move on. You do not matter to him at all. He sees you as an extension of himself, not an actual person and as such he wishes to possess and control you. That's it.

There is a school of thought emerging right now which postulates that all cluster B personality disorders (Histrionic, Borderline, Narcissistic and Antisocial) are actually just different levels on a narcissistic spectrum. This would mean that Antisocial Personality Disorder is simply the extreme end of the narcissistic spectrum. Since these disorders occur together very frequently and since they all contain some element of narcissism, this is a very plausible theory. It also shows us how destructive narcissism in any amount can truly be.

# THE WHY

The narcissist has a vicious, sadistic Superego (the part of a person's mind that acts as a self-critical conscience) that attacks him all the time with horrible, terrible things: "You're worthless, no one likes you, you're scum, you're a terrible person, there is nothing good about you..." They create a False Self to hide that, which is why they seem so arrogant, etc. But they are under attack by this Superego all the time, nearly every second, and so when they find a partner, this narcissist takes all that sadistic viciousness they are hearing from the Superego out on the partner to make themselves feel better. This is the only way they have to make themselves feel better and because of this, they are never going to stop doing it. You cannot make them see they are doing this; it's a defense mechanism. They have to believe their partner or others around them really are terrible people. It's essential to their whole being as a person and they cannot stop. More importantly, they don't want to stop. They are truly evil people who literally desire to destroy others because they are jealous and believe that other people have things (love, sex, material things, popularity) that they (the narcissist) are being purposely and spitefully denied.

There was a scene in Fight Club when Edward Norton's character beat the hell out of Jared Leto's character. The other guys asked him why he did it. He said, "I felt like destroying something beautiful"? That is the narcissist. The true narcissist is a dangerous, conscious-less, selfish, sadistic and evil person. And really, they are not truly people in the strict sense of the word. That is why a lot of people have the same reaction to narcissists as they do to very human-like androids. People can accept and even like androids, so long as they do not seem too human (like C3PO). But when an android seems too much like a human, people often react with revulsion, disgust and even fear or panic. This is called the uncanny valley hypothesis and it is the same reaction you often see to a narcissist; people aren't sure why they feel that way but something just feels "off" and it's a strong feeling, so strong that sometimes after just an encounter or two, people will stay away from the narcissist. This probably explains why even though he was good looking, smart, well-off and personable, Elliot Rodger could not get a girlfriend. This is the "alien" aspect of the narcissist and we see it over and over again; people can see that something is not right. They are sensing that the narcissist is a fraud and not a real human being at all. Others often cannot articulate what it is they don't like about the narcissist - who usually seems to be the picture of friendliness and sincerity - they just know they don't like it.

Read about any murder or crime where people were really hurt; chances are, you'll find one of these terrible humanoids at the bottom of it. Jails and prisons are full of narcissists. The only thing they care about is what they can use somebody for, and they will be whoever and whatever they have to be to get it. They don't care about other people's suffering or feelings; do you care how your couch feels when you sit on it? Do you wonder if you are being fair to your toaster? They are a true and accurate mimic, but don't be fooled. Narcissists are handicapped and crippled human beings in that regard: they have no real feelings at all for anyone other than themselves. And the scary thing is, they are almost sickeningly easy to create.

This brings us back to Elliot Rodger.

It's sort of sad how the focal point of that crime became gun control when the problem is so much more than that. We should be talking about how you create a person like that, because they absolutely are created. We need to stop teaching our children the value of things and start teaching them the value of people. We need to stop letting our children believe the world owes them something. We must stop giving them every single thing they want, and we need to stop rewarding selfish, self-absorbed behavior. We need to stop ignoring our children. We have to take time to be with them, to see them, to love them. We must teach our children love and the value of life. That is how we stop things like Elliot Rodger from happening. That is how we stop creating people like that.

Once they are created, it's too late. Medication cannot help them. Therapy cannot help them. Nothing can help them. They are what they are. And what they are is really nobody at all. They are shells walking through life seeking fulfillment, and the only way to get what they need is by using and abusing other people. They will go to whatever lengths they have to in order to get what they want. They see people as either stumbling blocks in their way or stepping stones to use. That's it and that's all. The narcissist will discredit you, lie about you, ruin your life, physically hurt you or even kill you in order to get you out of the way if he wants something bad enough.

# Why Narcissists Abuse

Narcissists are some of the most maligned people on the planet. While many other provocative personalities might evoke sympathy in people, the pathological narcissist does not. People may initially feel pity for the narcissistic personality - especially if he presents himself as a helpless victim, the way many narcissists do - but this is extremely short-lived because the narcissist is so controlling, abusive and hateful. It is nearly impossible to feel pity or sympathy for a person who works so hard to consciously and purposely hurt you. In fact, the narcissist seems compelled to hurt only those who love them, making it even harder to feel sympathy for them. But why? Why are narcissists so abusive?

## NARCISSISTS DO NOT VIEW PEOPLE AS PEOPLE

This can be hard for non-narcissistic people to understand. Of course narcissists see others as people. How could they not? But they don't. They know you are a person, just like they know a dog is a dog and a lamp is a lamp. However, that's where it ends; narcissists have no emotional connection to other humans, any more than a non-narcissist would have to that same lamp. People are viewed by narcissists as either objects to get to what the narcissist wants or as hurdles in the way of it. That's it. The pathological narcissist is unable to understand that other people have feelings. If they do understand, these feelings are considered totally unimportant when compared to the narcissist's own feelings and what they want. This is because the part of the brain that enables humans to care and empathize with other people is either missing in the narcissist or it's so dysfunctional and immature that it is completely ineffective.

Narcissists also enjoy manipulating, tricking and fooling people. It makes them feel smart and superior to have tricked or otherwise fooled people into doing, saying or acting the way the narcissist wants them too. This is made especially obvious by the way they will continuously provoke and insult someone - sometimes for hours - until the person reacts with anger, which the narcissist then reacts to by screaming that they are the ones being abused. If this is pointed out, the narcissist will flat out deny they've done anything wrong, insisting that they are the ones who are being mistreated.

# Narcissists Are Emotional And Psychological Vampires

These are people with no emotional lives of their own. They have no identities and because of this, they endeavor to steal other peoples' identity through a sort of "personality transplant." The narcissist has a very malformed and destructive self-image. They look in the mirror and see garbage, an ogre, an evil person who does not deserve to live. They resent anyone who is not as awful as they think themselves to be. They also envy that other person and want to steal all the person's good qualities for themselves. The only way the pathological narcissist can do this is to systematically degrade, demean and beat the person down nonstop until they don't have those good qualities anymore. If the person is caring, the narcissist calls them selfish. If the person is well -liked, the narcissist works to destroy the person's reputation and continuously tells the person all the reasons people don't really like him or her. If the person is smart, the narcissist works to humiliate them and make them look stupid. This is a crude form of brainwashing and a way to elevate themselves: if their loved one is stupid, the narcissist looks smart. If their loved one is told they are selfish, this means the narcissist is caring by comparison.

Of course, doing this does not transfer the good qualities to the narcissist as they'd hoped it would, but it is good enough for the narcissist to know that now nobody has the good qualities. In a very real sense, they want to bring everybody down to their level, because they feel desperately inadequate. They are unable to better themselves, so they choose instead to bring everybody else down. Their entire self-image is based on how they compare to other people, and since they always end up falling drastically short of even basic normal standards, the only way to boost their self-image is to drag other people down.

The narcissist effects the personality transplant not just by trying to steal someone's good qualities but also by forcing that person to carry all of the narcissist's bad qualities. This can only be achieved by repeatedly demeaning and degrading the person until they accept the things the pathological narcissist says as true. Once the narcissist has forced the victim to accept that the victim is a terrible, broken and evil person, the victim is then deserving of abuse for being terrible, broken and evil. The victim is forced to carry all of the qualities the narcissist hates about himself, and by doing so, the victim becomes the object of the narcissist's hatred.

# Narcissists Are Looking To Escape Punishment Themselves

The narcissistic personality is being assaulted and degraded, too - by himself. The pathological narcissist possesses a dysfunctional superego that savages him day and night with awful, terrible things about himself. He gets no rest from it. Every vicious, horrible thing he is saying to you is what he actually thinks of himself. That's why he says it. He is under attack 24 hours a day. The only thing he can do to try and get any respite from it at all is to attack someone else. These things aren't really true about him - they're true about you! You are the bad one, the evil one, the broken one, the human garbage. It's obviously true because he said so. Narcissistic Personality Disorder is, underneath it all, a set of malfunctioning defense mechanisms. The defense mechanisms that the child pre-narcissist needed to protect him from more damage have grown into pathological thought processes and behaviors. These defense mechanisms have turned on him and instead of protecting him, they now assault him nonstop with an endless tirade of how awful he is. At the same time, they prevent him from accepting or even hearing any criticism or taking any blame at all, ensuring that he will never be able to change. He really does think it's everybody else and he derives actual pleasure from punishing those he thinks deserve it.

This is why the narcissist is abusive; not only is he looking to simply pass the punishment along, but he believes himself to be so terrible that anyone who loves him must be irretrievably flawed themselves. The narcissist cannot accept any flaws in people who care about him; flaws render them a terrible, crushing disappointment to him. Since the very act of loving the narcissist convinces the narcissist that the person who loves him is hopelessly flawed, anyone who loves him is a target for his abuse just because they love him.

# NARCISSISTS ARE UNABLE TO CHANGE

As we can see, it is imperative that the pathological narcissist abuse his or her loved ones. It is literally interpreted by them as a life or death situation, and they belief they are acting in self-defense by abusing other people. For a narcissist to stop abusing their family members would be tantamount to emotional suicide. It would require the narcissist to admit that their needs are only as important as everybody else's needs, and to do that would be stating the narcissist's needs don't matter at all. It would be the same as being invisible. For a person whose every waking thought centers around how much attention they can get from other people, this is a fate worse than death.

# 5 Things You Should Know About Narcissists

Living with a pathological narcissist in your life is very painful. Far from just benignly in love with themselves as they are sometimes described, the true pathological narcissist is a brutal, sadistic manipulator and abuser. They are not only not in love with themselves, they cannot love anybody - including you. They will destroy your self-esteem, your reputation, your family, your support system, your dreams, your life and your very sanity if they get the chance, and for no other reason than they want to and they can. You represent everything they are not and can never be. They hate you for that and they will take it all away from you if you let them.

The best advice is to simply stay far away from narcissists once they've been identified in your life. Don't talk to them and don't feed into their manipulations. You can't help them. They cannot be saved. They can only pull you under with them - and they would truly love to do so. If the narcissist in your life cannot be avoided, here are five things to remember in order to protect yourself.

## 1. THE NARCISSISTS WILL ALWAYS USE YOU.

Narcissists are users. They are manipulators. They don't see people as living, breathing human beings with feelings. People are viewed as either stepping stones to get what they want or hurdles to be jumped over on the way to it. That's it. No matter what they tell people, no matter what they say, this is the truth. If we strip away their manipulative words and look only at their actions, we actually see this very clearly. It's who they are and it can never change. The part of their brain that enables them to care and empathize with other people is either missing or so dysfunctional that it is completely ineffective, depending on the childhood trauma that made them a narcissist in the first place.

Why do narcissists use people? Narcissists view people as objects and as extensions of themselves. Because of this, they are unable to see people as separate beings from themselves with their own feelings, needs, wants and opinions. We use our coffee pot. We use our arm. They are objects that serve a purpose in our life and nothing else. We don't worry about whether or not our arm wants to lift a gallon of milk. We don't think about if our coffee pot likes making coffee for us. We just make them do it. This is how the pathological narcissist sees and reacts to other human beings. Other people have things they want and they want to absorb these qualities into themselves somehow, to make up for what they are lacking. They will continue to use you for as long as they think you have something they want. They enjoy manipulating others and they get excitement and pleasure from tricking or "getting over" on other people. It makes them feel smart and superior.

This cannot be changed and it is very important that everyone dealing with a narcissist understand this. It's very tempting to view them as helpless, wounded children who need healing - especially the ones who present themselves this way - but narcissists are not children and they cannot be helped, fixed or healed. It is too late for them. It's very sad but the damage has been done. They are what they are and this cannot be changed. This cannot be changed. The narcissist cannot be forced to see other people as human beings. It is a waste of time to try to "get through" to them, or get them to see it. They are incapable of doing so.

# 2. The Relationship With The Narcissist Will Never Be Equal

This can be a hard one for people to accept. Most of us are raised to believe in equality and equal treatment for everybody, so when we run into someone who doesn't feel this way, it just does not compute. When dealing with a pathological narcissist, however, it is necessary to get this clear right away.

The relationship with a narcissist can never be equal. They don't want it that way. They don't want an equal relationship - at all. They want to be first. They need to be first and they will do whatever they have to do to ensure that they are the most important, the only one who matters. Any attempts the other person makes at independence and equal treatment are viewed as extreme threats by the narcissist and are reacted to as such. The person is attacked for daring to have feelings and for daring to think these feelings matter. The pathological narcissist cannot understand that other people have feelings and does not care anyway. All that matters to them is themselves. This may sound trite to some people, or cliché; we all know selfish people. Pathological narcissism is far more than just selfishness, though and anyone who has lived with a narcissist knows exactly how terribly abusive, how horribly painful and how destructive this kind of relationship is.

A person suffering from Narcissistic Personality Disorder can only be happy when they have crushed the other person beneath their feet. It is the only thing that makes them feel better about themselves. If they cannot control, dominate and crush the other person down, they will never stop trying and what results is an endless power struggle with the narcissist continuously accusing the other person of attempting to control, manipulate, oppress and subjugate them. In reality it is the narcissist who is doing these things, but they accuse the other person of it because unless the narcissist is the only thing that matters, they don't feel they matter at all. They cannot bear to be invisible and this is how they feel when they are forced to acknowledge other people's feelings, accomplishments or good qualities.

When dealing with a narcissist, it is imperative to always remember: they can only feel like a person by making other people feel like less than they are. They only feel validated when they can control and dominate others. This can never be any different. They will never see other people as equal. To do so would be the same as suicide for the narcissist. This is how important it is.

# 3. Everything The Narcissists Says Is A Lie, A Manipulation And A Scam.

It can be extremely difficult to extricate yourself from the relationship with a narcissist. They hang on very tightly. They can be charming and manipulative, desperate to keep control over you. It's hard to say no when they are saying all the things you have been waiting so long to hear from them.

Suddenly they've seen the light! You have shown them the way! It's finally happened! Losing you (well, almost losing you) was the kick in the rear end they needed to see how selfish they were being and Lord Jesus, it will never happen again! Saints be praised, it's a miracle!

No. It's a manipulation. Narcissistic lies are designed to trap other people into doing what the narcissist wants them to do. The lies narcissists tell are exactly what people want to hear and they are saying it because they know that. They know what you want them to say and they will say it if they have to, but it's never going to be true. Everything that comes out of these people's mouths is a lie. But why? Why do narcissists lie? They have no truth. All they have are lies and manipulations that go along with whatever they are trying to get you to do today. Tomorrow they will argue the exact opposite without batting an eye, if they have to do it in order to win. Winning is all they care about.

At 4 o'clock the narcissist is fervently apologizing for lying to you (again), saying he will do anything - anything, do you hear him?! - to make it up to you because he never meant to hurt you. You are the best thing that ever happened to him, you are amazing, you are wonderful. At 4:30 the narcissist is insisting he never lied to you. You claimed he lied and then forced him to apologize to you even though he's done nothing wrong because you are unreasonable, controlling and abusive. He twists everything that's been said in a way that makes it look like you are lying, confused or are deliberately making things up. When you continue to insist this isn't true or point out that he's already admitted to lying and apologized to you, he launches into a screaming hysterical tirade designed to control the situation by shutting you down and deflecting the consequences of his actions away from him. Look what you're doing to him! Look how you're hurting him! You cruel, evil, vicious abuser! Yes, OK, you think he lied and yes, OK, you did catch him red-handed in the lie but look at what you are doing! It doesn't matter what he's done! Nothing warrants this kind of abuse! YOU are the wrong one! YOU!

Why the change? He changes his tune because his initial tactic didn't work. You didn't do what he wanted you to do, which was accept his apology and simply forget that he lied with no hard feelings. The fact that it's the 30,000th time he's lied to you about the same thing doesn't matter to him. The fact that he is obviously not actually sorry doesn't matter to him, either. He's apologized and you need to accept it. If you don't, you're abusing him. He will continue to change his tactic until something does work. Apologizing didn't work, so now he changes to denial: he didn't really lie, you just think he did because you're stupid/crazy/unreasonable/controlling/etc. If this particular strategy doesn't work, he will change from attacking you to claiming you are attacking him: You're only saying he lied because you hate him so much. He can't do anything right or make you happy because you're cruel and abusive. When this tactic doesn't work, he reacts with a meltdown designed to guilt or frighten you into doing what he wants. This might entail violence - either toward himself or you, screaming, crying or any combination of emotional dysregulation.

Here is where something interesting often happens. If the final meltdown does not work, if you stand there and watch his hysterics stone-faced without backing down, he will calm down and start back at the beginning again and apologize. In fact, if the argument continues long enough, you will see him go through the same cycle of manipulation tactics over and over again. It's all he knows how to do. He can't take responsibility for what he's done (though he probably thinks his "apology" covers that), he cannot understand or care that he hurt you and he cannot see that he's done anything wrong. All he can do is try to control you by either telling you what he thinks you want to hear or using guilt, violence and hysteria to bulldoze you into what he wants. None of it is genuine, except for possibly the anger you see. Everything these people say is a lie designed to manipulate, control and force you to do what they want you to do.

However far he has to escalate it, whatever he has to do to control the situation and make you do what he wants you to do, that's how far it will go.

# 4. THE NARCISSIST WILL NEVRE CHANGE OR STOP ABUSING YOU.

Narcissists have a brutal superego that assaults them with horrible things 24 hours a day. Lashing out at other people is the only way they know to try and find peace from it. It doesn't work, but they have no other coping mechanism. They simply spread the misery around, hoping to take some of the punishment off of themselves. At the core of their personalities, narcissists believe they are bad. They believe they are weak, unlovable and broken. It is because of this that they treat the people who love them so badly. The very fact that the other person loves the narcissist must mean there is something wrong with that person. Because of this, the person is seen as irretrievably flawed and stupid, therefore deserving of the narcissist's abuse.

This is the nature of the relationship with a narcissist: it can literally never be anything but abuse. The other person only exists to make the narcissist feel better. In fact, the narcissist is hoping to effect a sort of personality transplant or swap with the other person. The other person is everything the narcissist feels he is not: caring, smart, charismatic, well-liked, competent, powerful, exciting...whatever. The narcissist wants to absorb those good qualities into himself and force the other person to carry all of his bad ones. He needs to control and dominate the other person in order to strip them of their coveted good qualities and take them into himself. He needs to abuse and reduce the person in order to force them to carry his bad qualities and relieve him of them. He is a weak person who cannot carry them himself and the image he projects of himself (and onto his victims) is nothing but lies.

That is another reason he is abusive: If he convinces the other person that they are bad - or convinces other people that the person is bad, that makes him good. If he lies about the other person and makes other people dislike that person, that makes him more well-liked. If he says the other person doesn't care, this means he cares more. If he convinces the other person they are crazy, that means he is competent. If he makes the other person feel weak, this makes him powerful.

This is who the narcissist is. This is why narcissists abuse. He projects all of his bad qualities on to other people, and when he is called out for doing these things, he simply says, "No, that's what you're doing. You must be the narcissist!" This results in a never-ending cycle of the narcissistic simply deflecting every single thing he is doing wrong onto the other person while never actually acknowledging or taking responsibility for any of it. He will never face reality. He can't. Narcissists are like the living embodiment of that old saying, "I'm rubber, you're glue. Whatever you say bounces off me and sticks to you!" Except they actually mean it. They live it.

Perhaps most importantly, the pathological narcissist enjoys hurting other people. Narcissistic abuse is like food to them, literally. They love it, because they hate themselves and they hate you. They get something out of hurting those who love them. They can't get it from just anybody. It has to be someone who cares about them; hurting strangers just isn't personal enough to give them that feeling that fixes them - even for just a second - and because of this, they are addicted to it. In fact, many times it is apparent how much they are enjoying themselves just by looking at them. They are often overconfident or unaware regarding how they appear to other people, so they make zero attempt to hide it.

If anyone reading this is waiting for the narcissist in their life to "see the light" or have that epiphany, give up now. It is literally essential to his well-being that he abuse, dominate and control others. He can never learn, he can never change and he will never stop. To stop abusing the other person would mean admitting that the person doesn't deserve the abuse and that's never going to happen. The other person now carries all of the narcissist's bad qualities and the narcissist absolutely despises these things. The other person is also seen as possessing good qualities the narcissist dearly wants and thinks he deserves but cannot have because the person cruelly refuses to give them. This is seen as very unfair, even abusive. The way the narcissist views it, he is striking back in self-defense because by not being given what he wants, he is being terribly, terribly mistreated. The pathological narcissist believes that a person who is that despicable, that abusive, that unjustly punitive and withholding toward him deserves all the abuse the narcissist can give them. And they will get it.

# 5. THE NARCISSIST CANNOT LOVE YOU.

If we've not made this apparent thus far, it needs to be apparent right now. If anyone reading this is asking themselves, "Can narcissists love other people?" the answer is no. The narcissist does not love you. You don't even love the narcissist, because the person you fell in love with (or want to love, if the narcissistic personality in your life is a parent, friend or sibling) does not exist. The person you fell in love with was a mask. It was a reflection of what you wanted and what you are. You essentially fell in love with yourself, because the narcissist was only reflecting your own wants and good qualities back to you in order to snare you. The real person is what is described here: a vicious, abusive, empty shell that needs constant sustenance, support and domination to exist.

The narcissist cannot be happy and they cannot let anyone else be happy, either. Even if you do absolutely everything the narcissist asks you to do exactly the way they ask you to do it and exactly when they want you to do it, they will find some way for it to be wrong so they can punish you. If you live with a narcissist, you probably already know that. Don't hold your breath or waste your time waiting for it to change. It won't. They are incapable of love, of empathy, of sympathy, of loyalty or of honesty. The "relationship" with a narcissist is an endless cycle of abuse, domination and cruelty. This never changes and it never ends. The narcissist cannot love anyone, especially themselves. They only know how to take.

25

# Are You Married to a Narcissist?

There are many kinds of people in this world, but perhaps none are so maligned as the pathological narcissist. Unfeeling, hurtful, sadistic, cruel and selfish, they are terrible spouses and disastrous parents. These people were never built to be caretakers. They are not capable of the love other people are capable of; indeed, many experts believe they are not capable of love at all.

If you are reading this, it's because you are concerned you may be living with a pathological narcissist. Please accept my deepest sympathies. You've probably already realized the person you thought you were in love with never even existed. It is imperative that you acccpt this, if you've not done so yet. You cannot change it. Your narcissistic partner cannot change it. It is what it is.

Here is a list of questions you can ask yourself to determine whether or not you could be living with a pathological narcissist. If you determine that you may be, you have a decision to make.

# DOES YOUR PARTNER SEEM TO BE TWO DIFFERENT PEOPLE?

He's the good guy in public, and a sadistic, vicious terror at home. Sound familiar? If it does, you could be living with a pathological narcissist. The narcissist is extremely concerned with what people think of him and in public he is often a model citizen. At home behind closed doors, he is unpleasant, nasty, cruel or even physically abusive. This can be for any reason - or no reason at all that you can decipher - but it is most often when he does not get his way or does not receive the admiration he feels he deserves. He reacts with unbelievable rage when criticized - or when he thinks he was criticized. (This is one of the many ways we can differentiate between narcissism and healthy self-esteem: a healthy person can laugh off, ignore or even logically evaluate criticism because he is secure; the narcissist cannot do this because he is not secure.) He can turn on you like a snake in an instant, savaging you with terrible, hurtful words designed to make you feel two inches tall. His anger is explosive and often way out of proportion to what has happened. Nobody else sees this side of him but you and your children. The side everybody else sees is the side you fell in love with. Unfortunately, you now know it's not who he really is.

There is another type of narcissist; this narcissist often wants sympathy instead of admiration and instead of appearing as the good guy in public, he portrays himself as a helpless victim and weak. No one would ever believe this poor pathetic wimp is abusive - but he is, behind closed doors.

# Does Your Partner Try To Manipulate Others Against You?

This is one of the hallmarks of the pathological narcissist. He lies about you to your family, friends and even your children. He spreads nasty rumors about you, he tries to humiliate you or shares your personal secrets all in an attempt to turn other people against you. The narcissist sees you as a rival for attention from these people and as such, he has to destroy your reputation so that they do not give you any of the love, admiration or attention he craves all for himself. He is jealous of any attention anyone else is given because he perceives others as better than he is. You are a good person who deserves love, admiration, respect and above all, attention. Deep inside, underneath all of his false ego, the pathological narcissist believes he is a bad person who does not deserve any of these things. Because of this, he desires to destroy your good qualities and "bring you down" to his level. Then he feels better because even though he doesn't deserve these things, now other people think you don't either. This makes him feel better and more in control because while he doesn't receive these things, now neither do you. This is especially horrible when children are turned against a parent simply because the other parent cannot stand that the children love that parent, too.

The weaker type of narcissist may not attempt to manipulate others against you in the same way. Instead of telling hateful, spiteful lies, they may tell lies designed to make them look like a victim and you look abusive but don't be fooled. This is not a case of "misunderstanding," or of a poor helpless little boy who just needs love and is acting out. The weak narcissist knows you are not abusive. He wants other people to think you are because he wants them to dislike you and feel sorry for him. Make no mistake about it: this is abuse.

# DOES YOUR PARTNER GASLIGHT YOU OR PLAY MINDGAMES?

Gaslighting somebody is the oldest manipulation trick in the pathological narcissist's book and they are very, very good at it. It's a form of crazymaking designed to make the other person feel unsure of reality. It keeps them off- balance and vulnerable to the narcissist's domination. It's a way of controlling the other person and the conversation.

## Examples of gaslighting include:

- ✓ "I never said that."
- ✓ "I didn't say that. You said that." "That didn't happen."
- ✓ "You're trying to confuse me." "You're imagining things."
- ✓ "You're crazy." "You're lying."
- ✓ "You're just saying that to hurt me." "You're making that up."
- ✓ "You're trying to frame me." "You're too sensitive."
- ✓ "I never hit you."
- ✓ "I didn't really hurt you."

It takes a very strong person to withstand repeated gaslighting. It's an insidious form of abuse that undermines a person's very perception and reality to the point that they become totally compliant with whatever the narcissist says. The truly evil part is that the pathological narcissist often claims - to you and to others – that you are gaslighting him. Again, don't be fooled; he knows very well who is manipulating who.

Does your partner blame you for everything?

Part of the way pathological narcissism works is that it prohibits the narcissist from accepting or even seeing when he is to blame. He blames you. Always. It doesn't matter how much he has to twist things to achieve this, he always achieves it.

"You made me hit you because you are always provoking me!"

"I wouldn't have to act like this if you weren't so __________!"

"I wouldn't have cheated on you if you weren't such a bitch!"

"I would not have lost my job if I wasn't always worried about what you're doing!"

"I was late for my appointment because you didn't wake me up!"

The pathological narcissist is a champion blameshifter. He not only blames you for things he does, but he blames you for everything bad that happens to him. The fact that it is not remotely your fault doesn't matter at all. The narcissist wants to punish you for things you haven't done because his disorder demands that he punish someone and he simply cannot stand for it to always be him. The pathological narcissist has a brutal, sadistic superego that beats him with internal criticisms 24 hours a day. Because of this, he literally leaps at the chance to take the punishment out on somebody else. It's the only escape from it that he has.

The narcissist cannot take responsibility for anything. The weak narcissist will often phrase blame statements as evidence of how you are abusing, manipulating and controlling him. He knows this is not true. He is saying it so that he does not have to admit that he is the abuser, the manipulator, the controlling one. If he had to admit that, his image as the victim would fall apart and he fears that more than anything. When his partner reacts to the constant provocation, cruelty and abuse with an angry outburst, he victoriously twists the situation around to claim he is the victim and his partner is the abusive one.

# DOES YOUR PARTNER ATTEMPT TO CONTROL EVERYTHING?

Narcissists are serious control freaks. They not only want to control their environment, they want to control everybody in it. They want to control everything about their partner: their thoughts, their feelings, their actions, their opinions, everything. The pathological narcissist takes any expression of individuality from their partner as a rejection and a threat; they actively try to stomp this individuality out of their partner as fast as possible. The partner is told their feelings are hurtful, their opinions are intentionally contrary to what the narcissist thinks or believes, their thoughts are offensive and their actions are bad.

Everything the partner does is twisted against them into something bad. All their motivations are painted as cruel, manipulative and abusive. Everything they do hurts or somehow upsets the narcissist unless it is exactly what the narcissist wants them to do. Even when the partner has done everything "right" or is in perfect agreement with the narcissist, the narcissist may suddenly decide their partner's actions, thoughts, feelings or opinions are wrong anyway, and punish their partner for it. The partner is left hurt, confused and unable to understand why the thing that was OK yesterday is suddenly wrong today, or why agreeing with the narcissist is not enough. This type of cruel unpredictable behavior keeps their partner completely off-balance and makes them easier to control.

By systematically picking apart everything that makes their partner who they are, the pathological narcissist eventually controls their partner completely. He may also use standard forms of control found in most domestic violence situations, controlling through violence, dominance, fear and tantrums.

The weak narcissist uses all of these methods but he also may attempt to control things through the appearance of neediness, clinginess and insecurity.

"I need to know where you are at all times. I'm too worried if I don't know."

"I can't deal with you being upset with me. It breaks my heart."

These statements look like neediness, but they are not. They are manipulations designed to control the other person and dismiss their needs as unimportant when compared to the narcissist's needs: "You're upset with me because you say I hurt you, but talking about what I did wrong is upsetting me and that's more important than how you feel." What a partner may initially perceive as insecurity is often revealed over time as utter selfishness - the narcissist's needs come first. Always. Many narcissists use this "weakness" tactic to escape guilt and blame. The victim is demonized and called cruel simply for having feelings.

# Does Your Partner Believe Everything Revolves Around Him?

Narcissists are completely self-absorbed people. They are selfish to the point of almost seeming inhuman. They cannot stand for the subject to divert from them, even for a second. They will either attempt to direct the subject back to themselves or they will simply tune out. The narcissist can offer no comfort, no sympathy and no shoulder to cry on. Any attempts to force them to talk about your problems results in either the narcissist "trumping" your problems with their own and making the conversation all about them, or with accusations that you only talk/care about yourself. Similarly, any anger or unpleasant feelings you have toward the narcissist are rejected as only existing to hurt them.

Narcissists do not appreciate your feelings as actual feelings; they can only see their partner's feelings as existing simply to affect them. It's like the entire world is a movie and he is the star. His boss calling a meeting to address "problems with the team" is really only talking about him. The landlord who insists on timely payment is only insisting because he doesn't like the narcissist. Everything that happens is connected to them somehow; that's why they believe everything you do is intended to affect them, in either a good or bad way. Pathological narcissists do not not see their partners as individuals at all. They see them only as external extensions of themselves. In fact, they see everything and everybody like that. This is why narcissists perceive everything as directly related to them: to them, it is. It's their world - literally. We are just living in it.

Does your partner feel he is entitled to whatever he wants?

Narcissists believe they should have whatever they want, regardless of whether they actually deserve it or not. They want unconditional love, admiration, respect... it doesn't matter that they are incapable of giving these things to other people. They want them all and, quite frankly, for their every wish, want, desire and whim to be granted. Now. If people do not acquiesce to this demand immediately, they are painted as abusive and unloving. In the mind of the pathological narcissist, want and need are inextricably confused, leaving the narcissist with the feeling that he is being rejected and denied necessary sustenance, even over small things that should not be important.

The pathological narcissist does not care if money is needed for bills or rent. He may spend all of it on things for himself if you don't stop him. If you try to stop him, you will face his rage and possibly physical abuse for daring to get in his way. There may be a huge blowup over a bag of chips or a pair of headphones, with the narcissist screaming that you are abusive, cruel, twisted and evil because he can't have them. You're denying him. You are - as usual – forcing him to settle for less because you want to oppress and degrade him. This is his way of controlling you. He uses abuse to get his way and he may routinely spend all the money to create catastrophes in order to keep the family in turmoil and hurt people.

He cares nothing for the needs of others. At all. All he cares about is what he wants.

Narcissists are often serial cheaters. They don't care how their partner feels. They only care what they want. They are often physically abusive as well, with the most abuse falling on the victim when she cannot do exactly what the narcissist wants at any given time. This is a lot of the time, because the narcissist sets his partner up in no-win situations where no matter what she does, it's wrong.

For example, the narcissist asks his wife to speak to his therapist. She doesn't know what to do, because if she does speak to the therapist, he will say she is trying to turn the therapist against him and sabotage his therapy. If she does not speak to the therapist, he will say she is trying to sabotage his treatment by "purposely withholding" important information. Either way, she is inviting abuse on herself simply by trying to do what he is asking.

He may tell his partner he cheats on her because she is "boring." When she reacts to this by trying to spice things up in the bedroom, he may laugh at her efforts or rage and call her a whore. Again, she invites abuse upon herself just by trying to do what he wants.

Narcissists believe they are special people. They often have very exact ideas about what they deserve or should have to do. It's very common for the narcissist to refuse to help around the house, work or do other things they consider beneath them. The reason for this is very simple: they don't think they should have to. Any attempts to get them to pull their own weight are met with explosive rage. How dare you try to turn them into your slave?! Who do you think you are?! You fascist Nazi dictator! The narcissist believes you should cater to him, and if you do not do so or if you attempt to create equality in the relationship, he will paint you as neglectful, abusive and uncaring. If the narcissist cannot have more than others, he feels that he is being horribly and maliciously slighted. He is not interested in equality at all. Not for himself and not for others. The narcissist is only interested in crushing others beneath his feet and whatever else can fill the emptiness that is inside of him.

# Does Your Partner Seem To Actually Like Hurting You And Ruining Things For You?

This is another hallmark of the pathological narcissist. He actually enjoys hurting others, and he enjoys destroying things that other people care about. Sometimes you can even see it in his face, when he's done or said something especially vicious to you. He will say or do the cruelest thing he can possibly come up with and then stand there drinking your reaction in like wine. It's disgusting to see but there is no mistaking it: he's enjoying himself. He likes how much it hurts you and how good it makes him feel to do it. In a way, he is addicted to it. It's the only thing that makes him feel better. This is extremely important to understand because this is the reason he will never stop.

So are you married to a narcissist?

If you've answered yes to all of these questions, then the chance is very good that you are indeed living with a narcissist in your home. This is a big deal, because regardless of what he tells you, it will never change. It will never get any better. He can never be any different. You have to accept that and resign yourself to the abuse if you want to stay in the relationship. Regardless of whether he is a weak narcissist (covert), a domineering violent narcissist (overt), or the manipulative smooth kind who is only controlling you for your own good because you're "too stupid" to do it yourself (overt), these things are abuse. Either resign yourself to it, or you have to leave the relationship. You cannot love him back to health. You cannot fix him. You cannot save him. You cannot stay, hoping it will get better. It won't. These are fundamentally broken people who don't want to get better.

Even if you aren't living with a pathological narcissist, your relationship is probably unhealthy at the very least and you should think about what you want to do going forward. Do you really want to spend the next 10 or 20 or even 30 years trying to please somebody who will never be happy? Do you want to spend the rest of your life with someone who does not value or care about your feelings in any way? That's no way to live.

# The Narcissists And The Empath

There is no more dangerous and painful relationship than a relationship with a Narcissist. These relationships are often categorized by abuse of every kind (physical, verbal, mental, emotional, financial... ), exploitation, gaslighting, manipulation and a total disregard for the other person by the Narcissist. We know Empaths to be kind, generous people who are plugged in deeply to other people's emotions, often knowing us better than we know ourselves. So why would an Empath be attracted to a Narcissist? Of course, a person does not have to be an Empath to be unlucky enough to have encountered the Narcissist. However, Empaths find themselves entangled with Narcissists a disproportionate amount of the time comparatively speaking and because it seems such an unlikely pairing in a lot of ways, this dynamic deserves some investigation.

NOTE: Though the use of the pronouns "he" and "she" are applied to Narcissists and Empaths respectively here, this is done only for ease of reading and should in no way imply that either personality can only be one gender. Narcissism and Empathic ability are not gender-dependent in any way.

## WHO IS THE EMPATH?

Empaths are people who are uniquely and exquisitely tuned in to the emotions of other people, even to the point of feeling these emotions. They are sensitive, kind and nurturing to a fault. They will unfailingly place the needs of other people before their own. This is a big reason they are attractive to narcissists.

# WHO IS THE NARCISSIST?

Narcissists are selfish, emotionally and morally bankrupt individuals who are unable to feel empathy for others in any true or meaningful way. They do not consider other people's feelings at all; indeed, they don't even realize other people have feelings in the same way that they themselves do.

It doesn't seem to make sense that two such people would be even remotely attracted to each other, let alone form what can seem to be an unbreakable, almost fatal attraction-type of bond, but it happens - and frequently. How, though?

# THE ATTRACTION

At first glance, it's easy to see why the Narcissist is attracted to the Empath. Empaths are everything the Narcissist is not: kind, caring, emotionally aware, supportive, in control, able to have relationships and make friends... True to his nature, The Narcissist covets things he does not have and he endeavors to take them from anyone who does have them (or at least ruin them so that no one has them). The Empath gives freely of herself, making herself a glowing beacon for the Narcissist. It's like waving a red flag in front of a bull. He senses an emotional source he can leech off of nearly indefinitely, like a battery that never dies. He can take and take and take, and in return she will give and give and give. This is the nature of the relationship between the two and it will never change.

But why is she attracted to him? In the beginning, the powerful "vibe" the Narcissist gives off will resonate very deeply within the Empath. It catches her attention, and she is drawn to him as magnetically as he is drawn to her because of it. His presence is often very emotionally intense and most Empaths are attracted to that, whether they realize it or not. He may also be hard to read emotionally (his vibe is intense but it may be very distorted, like static on a TV where one cannot see the true picture) and since reading other people's emotional states is often very easy for the Empath to do, she may be drawn to him in spite of herself in an attempt to figure him out. Who is this guy? What's going on with him? What's he about? In short order, he will reveal his lifetime of abuse (real or embellished) along with a carefully-crafted commercial pitch showcasing how wonderful he is (usually not real) - and how wonderful she is, even though he just met her - and she will be effectively snared because she does not realize at first that the intense emotionality she is reading from him has nothing to do with her. It is all for himself.

It would seem unlikely that the Empath would fall for this considering that she is very in tune with others' emotions and their true selves. Can't she see what he really is? The answer is yes, she can. Most Empaths sense something "wrong" about the Narcissist very quickly, sometimes during the first conversation. But she can also see something else, and it overrides everything else: how wounded and broken he is inside, beneath all the lies and abuse. He needs. It's not an act on his part or a mistake on the Empath's part; the Narcissist really is fundamentally wounded and broken inside. A large number of Narcissists are skilled at appearing helpless and lost.

That's because in many ways, they truly are. Her mistake is not in reading him wrong. Her mistake is in thinking she can help him.

This is the attraction. She wants to help him. It is her fatal blind spot, because the Narcissist cannot be helped and more importantly, he does not want help. Yet even when she can see this clearly, his wounds are clearer. They are evident in everything he does, even in the horrible things. Especially in the horrible things.

The Why

He is adept at making her believe she is the only one who can help him, or that she already has helped him. This is what she wants. It feeds her need to help, and no one is more convincing than the Narcissist when he is showering someone with praise or pushing their emotional buttons to get a response. She gives him the emotional sustenance he both wants and needs, allowing him to bask in the light of her care and attention all the time. It is a dangerously codependent relationship which revolves around superficially fulfilling the needs of only one person who can be neither satisfied nor happy. The Narcissist is like a cup with a hole in the bottom: no matter how much you pour into it, it is never enough.

There is an important distinction to make here, however. We say "superficially fulfilling" because it is important to remember that the Empath's needs are being fulfilled, too, even if this does not seem to be the case. She is usually the obvious injured party in the relationship but she is a willing injured party; she has locked herself in a situation where she can perpetually "help" someone who will always need her. She has made a "career" out of taking care of a professional victim who does not want to get better. This may seem like victim- blaming to some, but it is only by recognizing this very thing that the Empath can empower herself to get away from the

Narcissist for good: she has to understand that she is choosing to stay and she can choose to leave. He only has the power over her that she is giving to him.

Many Narcissists are arrogant overachievers but most are crippled by their disorder in many ways, unable to function in the world normally in more than a very superficial way. The Empath sees an opportunity to take care of someone in perpetuity - and even if she doesn't want to, her caring nature can make her feel that she must. What will he do without her? It doesn't seem fair to abandon him, regardless of how horrible he is because he is sick and the sickness is not his fault. It's true that the way his brain works is not his fault. Maybe no one loved him enough when he was a child. Maybe he was abused. Maybe none of it is really the Narcissist's fault. However, it is not the Empath's fault, either. She does not need to be punished forever because of someone else's mistakes. If she stays in the relationship with the Narcissist, she will indeed be punished forever.

This is the Empath's nightmare: abandoning those who need her when she could have helped.

That is the problem with her logic, though: she cannot help him. No one can.

# Empaths And Codependency

We hear a lot about empaths these days. There is an awakening happening in the world and a lot of people are experiencing things that they don't understand. There is often confusion, especially with things that are similar but not the same. Empaths and codependents fall into this category. While there are some similarities, they are generally different. Empaths who are unskilled or unable to control their receptivity can become codependents if they are not careful. Here we will examine the differences between the two and what you can do to heal from codependency.

## WHAT IS AN EMPATH?

Empaths are people who are literally able to feel the emotions of others. They are the opposite of a narcissist. They are nurturing, caring and sensitive. Empaths who are unaware of their gift might notice that strangers open up to them without solicitation, or that they can always accurately gauge the emotional "tone" of a room or situation. Empaths are often able to tell right away if someone is sad or if they are hiding something. In fact, it is not uncommon for empaths to be jokingly referred to as "human lie detectors." Empaths are not dependent on the other person or people for emotional sustenance, approval or validation. The bond that empaths create with others is sometimes called "telempathy," and it is usually associated with spiritual, psychological or physical healing.

# WHAT IS A CODEPENDENT?

Codependent people are reliant on others for their emotional sustenance. Codependents can be empaths and they can bond with others, but codependency has nothing to do with healing. In fact, codependency is a wound that needs healing. Codependency occurs when someone's needs are not being met and they become "merged" with another person in an attempt to meet them. It is often described as not knowing where they end and the other person begins. Codependency is unhealthy and dangerous, because the codependent sacrifices their own well-being for the other person. They often feel trapped or guilted into doing things they'd rather not do. Codependency is a largely self- inflicted problem, and it is very fixable in a non- personality-disordered person. Many times, enablers of mental illness and addiction have codependent problems. Codependency is sometimes seen as controlling or manipulative. It can be detrimental to the other person, such as in cases of a parent constantly giving money to a drug-addicted child. It is a prominent personality trait in the covert narcissist.

# WHAT IS THE DIFFERENCE?

As we can see, there are similarities between codependents and empaths. Both are extraordinarily sensitive to the feelings and needs of others, both are caretakers, and both are what we could consider "helpers," but there is a very big difference: codependency is destructive and harmful to a person and their relationships. Empathy is the exact opposite. There are other differences, too.

One of these differences is that empaths generally have healthy, strong boundaries between themselves and other people. Codependent people generally do not. This is what causes the inability to tell where they end and the other person begins. Boundaries are necessary in order to protect ourselves from unhealthy interactions or from being 'engulfed' by another person's personality and losing our identity, but codependents have a large amount of trouble with this.

Another difference is in how they respectively process another person's feelings and behavior. An empath will read the behavior and offer insight if needed or asked, but not feel personally affected. A codependent will feel responsible for the other person's feelings or behaviors. They are often unable to say "no" to things and have trouble separating their own feelings from the other person's. This is because of their difficulty with boundaries. When there is no boundary, there is no buffer or delineation between the self and the other person.

One of the biggest differences between the empath and the codependent is in goals and driving forces. The driving force of the codependent is often fear. Where empaths are generally able to communicate their feelings and boundaries clearly, codependents have a lot of trouble with this because they fear the other person's reaction and, more deeply, the possibility of approval and/or love being taken away from them as a result of not doing what the other person wants. This is a toxic situation that results in the codependent doing, saying or agreeing to things that they are not OK with.

We often find guilt at the bottom of the behavior as well. For example, the mother has meshed with the child emotionally; all she can see are his feelings. She feels guilty because she works so much and she feels this means she is not a very good mother, so she gives the child whatever he wants. She knows it is not productive or healthy but she cannot seem to stop and now whenever she does not give in, the child rages until she does. As the child gets older, he sees this underlying guilt and hits that button every time he wants something. When the mother says, "No, I will not give you money because you'll buy drugs with it," he says, "I wouldn't need drugs if I ever had a mother who was there for me! I hate you!" If she gives him what he wants, he will stop saying he hates her. Her son hating her is her worst fear come true and she simply cannot stand against it, especially because he is in so much pain on top of that. So she gives him the money, reinforcing the cycle for the thousandth time. She mistakenly believes that stopping her son's emotional upset - and her own - makes her a good mother. This is how the cycle continues.

The goals of the two personalities are different as well. Empaths are generally interested in healing and helping others, whereas codependents are interested in having their own needs met because they cannot do so themselves. The empath's end goal is generally "to help," whereas the codependent's end goal is generally "to be loved." Codependents often believe their goal is to help, but we can see the true goal in the way that codependents often support or enable behavior that actually hurts the other person (such as giving a drug addict money or making excuses for a partner's dangerous, risky behavior). These are things a healthy empath would not do. Empaths generally will not support or engage in emotionally unhealthy situations, but codependents often do. This is because the codependent mistakenly believes the ends justify the means. If they have to suffer in order to feel needed or loved, they will do it. This is a sign of hurt, not love, and it needs to be addressed.

Codependents often suffer from self-image and self-esteem problems. They may believe someone will not love or like them if they do not sacrifice unfairly, or they may feel that they have no value without the other person. Again, this is a sign of a wound that needs to be healed. Approval and validation from others should not be so important that a person will cause themselves harm to get it. We see this in Borderline Personality Disorder all the time, as well as the manipulation of other people because of fear. Manipulation of others through deceit or withholding of feelings is still manipulation, and even if it seems harmless or "for the greater good," it isn't. Relationships need honesty and boundaries to be healthy.

# WHAT CAN YOU DO?

Empaths generally become codependents when they do not have good boundaries established. Strong boundaries are essential for everybody but they are imperative for the empath. Because the empath feels things so deeply, there needs to be a clear line between the self and other people, our own feelings and other people's feelings, our own personalities and other people's personalities. When these boundaries are blurred or don't exist, enmeshment occurs - and enmeshment is very strong with an empath. This is the dynamic between the empath and the narcissist. It is an unhealthy, unsustainable situation where both parties end up feeling trapped and unhappy.

Even if the empath is not a codependent, they may become enmeshed with a codependent if boundaries are not kept strong and inflexible. Codependents such as pathological narcissists will push for enmeshment because they don't feel secure without it. This must be guarded against and boundaries are how we do that. This is why it's very important to not fall victim to what's called "boundary ambivalence." This happens when we set a boundary but we don't enforce it. It tells the other person that we are not really serious about respecting ourselves and they don't have to be serious about respecting us, either. When you say, "If you cheat on me again, I'm leaving you" but you stay in the relationship when they cheat on you again, you have shown your partner that you don't really mean what you say and that you are not to be taken seriously. You are essentially saying, "I don't respect myself and you have permission to treat me badly." People only treat us the way we allow them to treat us. If you don't take your word seriously, nobody will and no relationship is worth your self-respect.

If you worry that you might be codependent, take a personal inventory. Why are you in this relationship? Do you feel you are sacrificing for others all the time? Are you able to meet your own needs or are you relying on the other person to do this for you? Do you speak up when you are unhappy with something or don't want to do something? Are you always feeling trapped or guilted into things you don't want to do? Do you feel taken for granted, or that you always need to fix everything? Do you anticipate the needs of others? This in particular is a red flag for codependency. Empaths generally do not attempt to learn what others need and supply that for them, but codependents do this often.

It is important to identify the problem - as well as your role in the problem - so that you can work on the solution. Again: people only treat us the way we allow them to treat us. Denial is very common with codependency, but we are responsible for our own behavior and our own feelings, so accepting your role in the problem can be difficult but it is necessary. If you are not prepared to do that and to be really honest about it, you are not prepared to heal from codependency.

# In order to begin healing from codependency:

Identify the problem and your role in it take avery honest inventory of yourself to find out why you are codependent Address unresolved issues from your past Work on setting boundaries and sticking to them Work on self-esteem and self-image Work on identifying and meeting your needs yourself Work on saying what you mean and meaning what you say Learn to let go of guilt remind yourself that you are not responsible for the actions or feelings of others Practice assertiveness.

# Get therapy if necessary

For empaths and other caretakers, it can also be necessary to find another area to focus your empathy on where you do not feel taken advantage of. A situation where you are not so personally involved such as volunteering can do wonders for changing perspective and fulfilling that "need to help." Just remember going forward that it is necessary to protect yourself from the emotions of others, otherwise the problem cannot be resolved.

If you have trouble setting boundaries, practice, practice, practice. Look in the mirror and say, "I don't like that, and I will not tolerate it" or maybe, "No, thank you, I have other plans." Try out being assertive in situations that you find yourself in. You will be surprised how many people can take a "no" without getting upset. If someone does get upset, remember that it is a reflection of who they are, not who you are. You have the right to your own feelings and your own needs, and anyone who does not respect that is not someone who should be in your life.

# How Empaths Can Protect Themselves From Anxiety & Depression

Being an empath in today's world is very difficult. The world these days is cruel, cold and brutal. However, it is also beautiful and amazing, and the key is to never lose sight of the good when we feel overwhelmed by the bad. Not everybody is an empath, of course, but we can all use a little protection from the emotional battering of the world in it's current incarnation.

## PAY ATTENTION TO WHAT YOUR BODY IS TELLING YOU.

Most modern medicine is about silencing the body. We hear how we have to push through the pain and keep on even when we are exhausted. We take supplements or ingest chemicals like caffeine designed to silence, mask or alter what the body is trying to tell us. We may feel this to be necessary sometimes, but it is almost always a mistake. Aches, pains, irritability, chronic illness and feeling tired are warning signs that your body and your mind have had enough. Don't ignore them. Take time when you need to and learn to say "no." This is often the empath's biggest obstacle; it is very difficult to turn people away when we know we can help, but you are no good to anyone if you are not well. You cannot take care of anybody without first taking care of yourself.

# AVOID TOO MANY CHEMICALS OR SUGARS

A lot of times, being an empath means dealing with overstimulation. Chemicals like caffeine, additives, artificial colors and sugars can make overstimulation much worse, leading to anxiety and other problems. Cut out the caffeine and the sugar as much as possible.

# GET ENOUGH SLEEP.

This seems like a no-brainer, but how many of us actually get enough sleep? Not getting enough sleep is often treated as no big deal, but it has been proven to have the same effect on you as a .05 blood-alcohol content. This dulls reaction times, affects accuracy with tasks, makes us irritable and causes things to bother us more than they should. Empaths need to have all pistons firing correctly if we want to be able to deal with what the world is throwing at us, so be sure to get enough sleep. How do you know you've gotten enough sleep? Your body will let you know.

# MEDITATE.

We probably hear this too much, but the benefits of meditation cannot really be overstated. Studies have proven that meditation works as well or better than psychiatric drugs for combating anxiety, depression and other problems. It can be difficult to do at first, especially with our society's limited attention spans but it is worth it to keep trying. Even if you don't feel like anything is "happening" while you meditate, your brain and your body are benefiting from the relaxation and over time, you will notice a change.

# REMEMBER TO BE GRATEFUL.

This one is not as easy as you might suppose. Think about it: in the course of one day, how often do you just feel simple gratitude? How often are you grateful for what you have, or just grateful to be alive? It can be very difficult to remember good things when we are under a constant barrage of negativity from all sides. It's everywhere, and we can very easily be pulled down into despair over it if we don't remind ourselves that there is good out there, too. Easy ways to do that would be to look for stories of people helping each other, writing down 5 things you are grateful for every day and saying them out loud, helping others who are less fortunate (gratitude is contagious!), remembering times when you yourself were less fortunate and how it got better... There are so many things to be grateful for in this life. Don't forget any of them.

# LET YOURSELF BE AMAZED.

We take many things for granted in this life, but if we really think about them, so many of them are truly amazing. Everything from the compact disc to the human hand has it's own wonder. How often do you think about it?

# GET BACK TO NATURE.

One of the biggest reasons people are so stressed nowadays is that they are living lives they were not made for. Humans were not created to work, sleep and die. We are wonderfully, beautifully, amazingly complex emotional creatures capable of a huge spectrum of behavior and emotion. We live very unnatural lives compared to our ancestors and taking time to reconnect with that is very beneficial for the mind, body and spirit. Put the phone down. Turn off the TV. Go for a walk. Go camping. Go barefoot! You may have heard of "earthing," which is walking barefoot on the earth in order to ground and balance your body. There is an entire science behind this and it feels wonderful regardless. (This is also called "grounding" in reference to our body's electrical systems and grounding is very important for empaths to do.) Get some fresh air and really give yourself time to be alive for a while. You'll be amazed what a difference it makes.

# VISUALIZE PROTECTION FOR YOURSELF.

If you find yourself in a situation that is overwhelming you (such as a place where there are a lot of other people, or when dealing with an emotional vampire), the best protection is in your mind. Empaths and sensitive souls receive other people's emotional vibrations like an antenna. This can make being around large groups of people difficult and exhausting, even scary or frightening. The way to beat it is to block the reception of this energy. Before entering the situation, close your eyes and visualize the energy being blocked from you. You can visualize an impenetrable shield or bubble around yourself that energy cannot get through. You can visualize an antenna retracting back into your mind so that it is no longer capable of receiving people's emotional output. You can visualize a door closing and blocking access to the recesses of your mind, a cord being unplugged, a ribbon being cut... Whatever visualization appeals to you, you can use and it will work. There is no wrong way to do it. It can take some practice to get it down pat, but the important thing is that the visualization be strong. If you are already in the situation and feel overwhelmed, you can either go into a quiet area and do it or simply concentrate hard right where you are. It does not take long and you should feel some release from the pressure of other people's minds immediately.

# LEARN TO SAY NO.

This bears repeating. Remember: you don't owe anyone anything. Of course we are tasked with helping others; that's why we were created as empaths. This does not mean that we are supposed to help others to our own detriment. Narcissists and other emotional leeches love empaths. They seek us out, because we are like psychic batteries to them, and they will hang on draining us until there is nothing left if we do not stop them. Helping others is never supposed to be a burden. Listen to yourself and learn when enough is enough.

It isn't easy being an empath these days but it is so rewarding. By learning to ground and protect yourself, you are making life better for not only yourself but for those you are charged with taking care of in this lifetime.

# Covert vs Overt Narcissists: What is The Difference?

Narcissists are people who are focused only on their own needs. They are unable and unwilling to care about or consider other people's feelings. They don't understand respect, integrity or compromise. They want what they want, when they want it and anything (or anyone) that stands in their way is their enemy. The true narcissist is remorseless, selfish, sadistic and shallow. Narcissists can be any age, gender, sexuality or race.

## WHAT IS AN OVERT NARCISSISTS?

When we think of narcissists, we usually think of arrogant blowhards who believe they can do no wrong, or that they are God's gift to humanity. This is the Overt Narcissist. He is overtly narcissistic. "Overt" means plainly seen or not hidden. This describes the Overt Narcissist exactly. He is arrogant, egotistical and not afraid to toot his own horn. In fact, he revels in it and insists that everyone else should do so, too. He may be sarcastic, sadistic, condescending, cruel and cold. This is not a sympathetic character. He will rage when challenged and he insists that his needs be catered to immediately. Any and all individuality in a partner will be brutally cut out and replaced with his way of thinking. He is often a bully, a cheater and it is not uncommon for him to engage in physical abuse of his partners. He believes he is entitled to literally anything he wants; this is the person who makes unbelievable statements of entitlement with a straight face. His selfishness is shocking and scary. He is often very smooth and seems to have things very together.

This type of narcissist is very dangerous but they are also very obvious. It's pretty hard to mistake this type of personality. They do everything but shove it in your face. Overt Narcissists often perfect a smooth facade to attract partners or friends but this facade generally crumbles pretty quickly, because that huge, poisonous ego demands acknowledged now. Because of this, they are, in some ways, easier to avoid than their counterpart, the Covert Narcissist.

# WHAT IS A COVERT NARCISSISTS?

The Covert Narcissist is the opposite of the Overt Narcissist. "Covert" means hidden or secret. This is a perfect definition for the Covert Narcissist. He does not appear to be a narcissist at all. Rather, he appears very insecure, helpless and needy. Where the Overt Narcissist appears supremely confident and independent, the Covert Narcissist presents himself as unsure and dependent. He is a very sympathetic, pitiable character. He makes sure to present himself that way.

The Covert Narcissist is a professional victim. He has had the hardest life, the roughest childhood, the most terrible relationships... his entire existence has been one tragedy after another. No one has ever loved him. Everyone has always left him. He tries so hard but it never works out. He clings to his partner with a desperation that is almost obsessive. This type of narcissist is very dangerous, because people do not recognize him as a narcissist. It is only after knowing him for a while that people begin to realize how selfish and self-absorbed this person really is. What we mistake for insecurity is actually selfishness - his needs come first. Always.

This is generally the type of narcissist that empaths become entangled with. This type of narcissist broadcasts his neediness like a beacon and it attracts people who want to help. He is like a predator feigning an injury in order to trick the prey into coming closer. This type of narcissist is still a predator, and in some ways he is worse than the Overt Narcissist because the Overt Narcissist makes his victims believe they need him, but the Covert Narcissist makes his victims believe that he needs them. Where the Overt Narcissist uses bullying and fear to keep his victim in line, the Covert Narcissist uses sympathy and guilt. This is much harder for victims to walk away from, especially because the Covert Narcissist appears so needy and unstable.

# WHAT IS THE DIFFERENCE?

Strictly speaking, there is not much of a difference between Covert and Overt Narcissists. It is mostly a matter of degrees. The Covert Narcissist attempts to have his needs met differently than the Overt Narcissist, but his needs are basically the same and have the same importance. The only importance, as far as he is concerned. The Covert Narcissist may cry hysterically or threaten suicide instead of physically attacking his victim or threatening murder (as the Overt

Narcissist would probably do), but they are both sides of the same coin. In this scenario, both people are saying the same thing: someone is going to die if you don't give me what I want.

In extreme emotional situations, both types of narcissists can engage in physical abuse and both can become hysterical or threaten suicide. This is because both the Covert and the Overt Narcissist are really only facades anyway. This facade can be cast aside if necessary to expose the wounded, screaming child underneath, and in both people this core is the same.

How they choose to present themselves has more to do with what their original personality was like before they received the narcissistic wound that made them what they are and with what they have learned works as a successful manipulation. The Overt Narcissist learned early on that bullying works better for him - probably because it is more natural for his personality type, and the Covert Narcissist learned that guilt and sympathy work better for him, probably again because it is more natural for him.

It can also have to do with which personality disorder the narcissist is afflicted with. We could then say that Borderline Personalities are more likely to be Covert Narcissists, whereas Psychopaths are more likely to be Overt Narcissists. Both are still narcissists, they are just different types. This is complicated by the fact that most people with Cluster B personality disorders have more than one, which will result in different types of behaviors coming out at different times.

For example, if a person has Borderline Personality Disorder, Narcissistic Personality Disorder and Antisocial Personality Disorder, this person may show many signs of Covert Narcissism but can also show signs of Overt Narcissism in certain situations. He may cry and threaten suicide when upset but if he feels insulted, he may respond with physical violence or death threats. These types of behavior do not seem to jibe at all with the "I'm helpless, I'm a needy child, I'm toxic waste, I'm scum, I'm a victim" mindset, but it happens because the core of every type of narcissism is a huge, poisonous and defective ego. This ego demands acknowledgment and it demands punishment when it is wronged.

In this regard, there is no difference at all.

# Are Psychopaths Actually Narcissists?

nyone who has been unfortunate enough to encounter a psychopath will tell you that psychopaths are the most selfish people on the planet. They care literally nothing for other people. All they truly care about is what they want. Seeming to have no genuine feelings of their own, the psychopath is like an empty machine which can only fill it's own wants and endlessly hunger for more. This is not so different from the way the pathological narcissist behaves. So how similar are they? What's the difference?

## THE SCIENCE

Both psychopaths and narcissists suffer from what is called "the narcissistic wound." This is the defining injury to the psyche which occurred during the young psychopath or narcissist's development. It is the trauma or series of traumas that made them what they are.

In the narcissist, the trauma(s) occurred after some emotions developed butbefore regulation of these emotions or empathy was learned. Therefore, we could say the narcissist suffers from "too much" emotion, rather than not enough. The emotions he does possess are out of control and unregulated because he is unable to control them, much the same way a very young child is unable. The narcissist's emotions are all self-focused however - again like a very young child - and if he possesses empathy at all, it is generally maladaptive and dysfunctional. His few emotions are simply too important; they are the focus of his entire being. It is for this reason that he is unable to empathize with other people. Other people just don't matter as much as how he feels.

In the psychopath, the narcissistic wound occurred before any truly genuine feelings developed at all. Therefore, for all intents and purposes, the psychopath has no real feelings. These feelings have never developed and they never will. There is no empathy, dysfunctional or otherwise - even for himself. He may feel primitive variants of fear or anger (the kind all animals feel to ensure self-preservation, like fight-or-flight), but many psychopaths don't even feel those. There is literally nothing there. They only feel "physical feelings," such as when something feels good to the body and they can become addicted to these things because it is the only experience they have with "real" feelings. This is the dynamic we see at play with serial murderers and psychopaths that are adrenaline junkies.

# THE DIFFERENCE

In relating to other human beings, there are some differences between the psychopath and the narcissist, and there are many similarities. The main difference seems to be in interpersonal relationships. The pathological narcissist and the antisocial personality are both manipulators and both wear masks. However, the narcissist needs other people very much. The psychopath does not. Unencumbered as he is by the emotional baggage carried around by the narcissist, the psychopath can play out a role for a very extended period of time if he must. He can derive private satisfaction from his wrongdoings, without relying on external validation of how powerful he is. This is something the narcissist has a lot of trouble with; his true self always comes through in the end, because it demands acknowledgment and it demands satisfaction - loudly. His end goal is purely selfish. The psychopath's goals are selfish as well, but they do not rely on the validation of others. Because of this, his ego does not come in to play the same way the narcissist's ego does and the psychopath can remain "hidden" for far longer. In fact, unless he makes a very serious mistake (which is rare but does happen), he may never be revealed.

The difference between psychopaths and narcissists then, is one of degrees. We could say that a psychopath is an "end stage narcissist." When narcissism is taken to the nth degree and the personality is so self-involved and self-focused that literally the only feelings which may occur are those aimed at making the self feel good, you have a psychopath. This is why there is so much overlap: psychopaths are narcissists. Many narcissists have antisocial tendencies as well.

# THE THEORY

In healthy people, there is a level of narcissism but it is not pathological. That means that it isn't inflexible. Healthy narcissism does not demand that others worship, revere, admire or give things to the person just because the person wants these things. Healthy narcissism does not scream that it's being oppressed or abused just because the person can't have what they want. People with healthy amounts of narcissism do not insist that others go without so that they can have more. People with healthy amounts of narcissism do not insist that you must set yourself on fire to keep them warm - and that if you won't, you are abusive and uncaring.

This graphic shows the whole narcissistic spectrum for human emotion and personality. As we can see, cluster B personality disorders are grouped beneath "pathological narcissism."

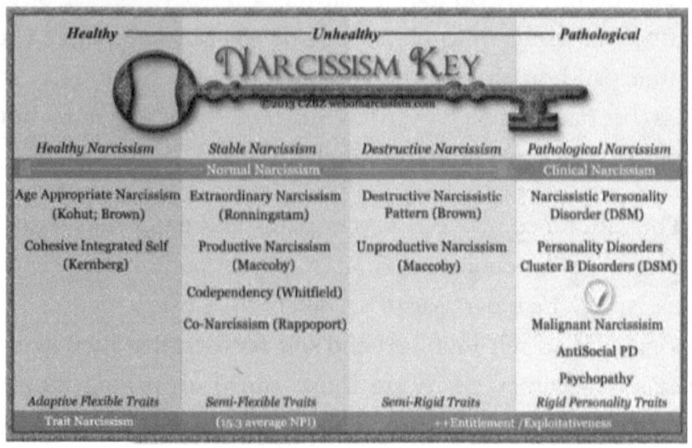


As seen in the above graphic, there is a theory which postulates that all cluster B personality disorders sit on a "pathological narcissistic spectrum." This is a theory which carries a lot of weight. The cluster B personality disorders are: histrionic, borderline, narcissistic and antisocial. If we were to envision the spectrum of malignant narcissism to start at histrionic personality disorder and end with psychopathy, we can see that there is indeed quite a bit of validity to this theory.

Note that this particular spectrum does not encompass all narcissism, as the first one did. This second graphic measures malignant narcissism, or pathological narcissism. All of the cluster B personality disorders express some type of pathological narcissism. The further down on the spectrum someone is placed, the worse the pathological narcissism is, until we arrive at Antisocial Personality Disorder, which is the complete absence of empathy or conscience.

Notice that there is not a large gap between Narcissistic Personality Disorder and Antisocial Personality Disorder. This is because there is a great deal of overlap in these. It is interesting to note that most of the cluster B disorder do occur in "clusters;" that is, they rarely exist on their own. There is almost always another cluster B personality disorder that is co-morbid. Many people will be diagnosed with HPD, NPD and BPD. Or they may be diagnosed with BPD, NPD and APD. This is another signal that the "narcissistic spectrum" theory is right on the money.

There is more than one type of psychopath and another interesting thing to note is that the further down the spectrum a person is placed, the fewer symptoms of the other cluster B personality disorders are present. You wouldn't expect a psychopath to go into the hysterical tizzies that Borderline Personality Disorder is famous for, and most of them don't. This can probably be attributed to psychopaths having no true emotions. If a psychopath were to have such an emotional outburst, it would serve you well to investigate if it's an act first, before concluding that it's genuine. It probably isn't. Histrionics, Borderlines and Narcissists feel cheated, overlooked and discarded by the rest of the world. The psychopath just doesn't look at things that way. As the quintessential narcissist, it is impossible for the true psychopath to feel anything about or for other people at all. This usually includes anger.

The idea that psychopaths are "mad at the world" is interesting but really a misnomer; they feel nothing for the world or the people in it. The difference between this and the narcissist is that the psychopath generally feels nothing for himself either, whereas the narcissist feels only for himself 95% of the time. Most psychopaths don't fear death, illness or injury (whereas many narcissists fear these things greatly). This could be because - as some experts have stated - psychopaths are never even really alive in terms of human existence.

# Are Narcissists & Psychopaths Evil?

In today's society, it is very common to hear the term "evil" thrown around, but what does it really mean? If you ask five different people, you'd likely get five different definitions. For the purposes of this discussion, we are going to use "evil" as both a noun and an adjective. For example, we would say that a demon is evil in both senses of the word. A demon engages in evil behavior, a demon is an evil being. A demon therefore does and is evil. The word both describes them and defines them.

Psychopaths and pathological narcissists often engage in evil behavior, but are they evil beings?

Can people be evil?

# EVIL IN THE REAL WORLD

The word "evil" used to conjure up visions of devils and demons. Now, it usually brings to mind a more human breed of evil. More than one psychologist has flat-out stated that some people are just evil. They are born evil and they stay that way until they die. Nothing will change them or make them better, largely in part because they don't want to be better. "Evil" is often the only way to describe a person whom psychology cannot explain.

Jeffrey Dahmer is one such example. There were no terrible incidents of abuse in his childhood, no severe head injuries... His brain was examined after his death and found to be perfectly normal. There is no real scientific explanation for Damher's behavior at all. He was a mystery, psychologically-speaking - to science and even to himself. Dahmer stated on more than one occasion that he did not know why he was the way he was, or what made him that way. Narcissists and psychopaths are not usually overflowing with personal insight, but it's rare for anybody (even a narcissist) to have absolutely no idea why they did something. He was able to offer no explanation at all.

There are some murderers whose eventual behavior can be, if not predicted, at least foreseen. We can look at a history of abuse, abandonment and neglect and say, "I can see how this person could have become a killer." Dahmer does not fit into this mold. All things considered, he should not have become a serial killer. But he did. Why?

Nobody knows. Dahmer is not the only example of this phenomenon, of course. He is a better-known example, and his atrocities are common knowledge but he is not the only example by far. So how does this happen?

There could be two explanations for this phenomenon, one scientific and one spiritual. Science defines evil as the absence of something, and spirituality defines evil as the presence of something.

# SCIENCE

If we are defining evil as the absence of humanity, as science is wont to do, then we could explore the idea that because psychopaths and narcissists are largely empty inside, this empty space must be filled up with stimulation. As they are also very damaged individuals, both pathological narcissists and psychopaths are consumed with the concept of power. Many of them were severely abused as children and the idea of having power is very important to them, as they seek to counter a lifetime of feeling like helpless victims. They were taught that the way to have power is to hurt other people. Therefore, the idea or process of achieving power is very important to the type of stimulation they will seek. When the innate cruelty of the narcissist and psychopath is added to the mix, you have a very dangerous individual on your hands. According to this definition, psychopaths and pathological narcissists are evil because they lack humanity. They lack many things, in fact: empathy, a conscience, insight...

This theory is mostly sound as far as it goes, but for the people who do not have histories of abuse, it simply does not make sense. We can easily see how most narcissists and psychopaths are created. It is understandable that someone who is abused would spend a lifetime trying to get over it or striking back against it any way they could, and it is understandable that constantly hurting or humiliating a child will create an adult who is very angry and has no empathy toward other living things. It is therefore correct to assume that it is both nature and nurture which generally create the psychopath and the narcissist: without the "perfect storm" of both environment and predisposition, people generally do not become psychopathic or pathologically narcissistic. What about the others, though? The ones who do not seem to have been created, but born that way? How do we explain that? These people do exist and we don't understand why.

# SPIRITUALITY

If we are defining evil as a supernatural presence, as spirituality is wont to do, then we could explore the idea that because psychopaths and narcissists are largely empty inside, something malevolent simply "moves in" to the empty space and begins exerting influence. The narcissist and the psychopath have malfunctioning defense mechanisms and are inherently weak; they would be an ideal target for a malevolent squatter. They are also less capable of insight and very susceptible to distorted perception, flattery and appeals to vanity. This can make them easy to manipulate or trick, another thing which flags them as ideal targets. Lastly, most narcissists and psychopaths are disproportionately preoccupied with power. This often results in dabbling in demonology and similar things, making them more likely than others to blatantly invite a dark energy into their lives. A person with no absence within them may not be affected by "messing around" with something like that, but the psychopath and narcissist are far more susceptible.

The spiritual theory of presence, though perhaps unlikely to many, would seem to explain a few things that science cannot, including the curious phenomenon of psychopathic children.

# THE BORN PSYCHOPATH

Science does not allow the labeling of these children; they cannot be considered psychopaths until they are adults. This has no bearing on reality, however. They are psychopaths and they appear to be psychopaths since birth. It's important to note here that there is no history of abuse with these children. Studies show that the parents of these "cold children" (as they are called) are as involved and loving as the parents of normally -functioning children, but the cold child does not respond as the normally-functioning child does. The cold child does not recognize or seem to care about the love he is being shown. It does not interest him. He displays sustained rages, continual aggression, calculated violence and calculated cruelty - even at four and five years of age. He does not fear consequences or social ramifications ("If I'm a mean person, others won't like me"), he is remorseless and he lacks empathy completely.

We could argue that children of that age don't necessarily understand empathy, and most people would argue that. However, the behavior of these particular children says differently. Calculated violence and cruelty display an active, conscious intent to cause harm. This means the child understands their actions are hurtful - and that being hurtful is the goal. This is both an acknowledgment and a denial of empathy: the child understands empathy and chooses to reject it in favor of causing harm. Why? Because though he apparently understands empathy, he obviously does not feel it.

These children have no emotional empathy, but as they mature, they develop the ability to simulate interest in people's feelings; a sort of cognitive empathy. They can say what other people feel and recognize it after a fashion; they just don't care or feel it. They understand intellectually that people have feelings, but that is as far as it goes. Other people's feelings have absolutely zero value or meaning to them. This is identical to the way adult narcissists and psychopaths behave. The manipulative and calculating behavior seen in these children generally far exceeds what a child their age should be capable of engaging in, as well.

There are many scientific theories for why these children exist at all, most involving hormones or genetics, but as of yet none have panned out. The current theories do not explain why some of these children do such terrible things while others don't, however, and certainly, hormones and genes do not even come close to explaining how a child under 10 years old is able to reason and calculate as if they are an adult.

Perhaps science is just not going to be able to explain that.

# SCIENCE VS. SPIRITUALITY?

If, as we said, science defines evil as the absence of something, and spirituality defines evil as the presence of something, this would seem to put the two theories at odds. But does it? Something can only establish a presence in an already-existing absence. This means that the spiritual theory actually fits in with the scientific one perfectly, and it's quite a bit older than its scientific counterpart. In order for something to fill a vessel, the vessel must be empty. You cannot pour more water into a full bucket. The scientific community generally stops short of considering a presence of any kind, but it acknowledges that evil does exist and admits that evil cannot be explained by science - at least currently.

Perhaps it is a mixture of the two, rather than one or the other. The "nature vs. nurture" debate raged for years before both sides gradually came to the realization that both nature and nurture contribute almost equally to any psychological situation. There are more things in the universe than can be explained or even experienced, and science readily admits this as well. It is not such a hard leap then, to theorize that perhaps in this absence that exists in the narcissist and the psychopath, something else might come to be.

Regardless of which theory one subscribes to, it can be said that according to science, the narcissist and the psychopath are indeed evil.

# Narcissists, Borderlines & Psychopaths: How to Stop Gaslighting

If you are not familiar with the term "gaslighting," it originated from an old movie starring Ingrid Bergman entitled Gaslight. In the movie, a man attempts to drive his wife crazy by manipulating her surroundings, then claiming her perception of the manipulated surroundings is mistaken or delusional. In the movie, when the lights dim because of something he is doing and she comments on it, he says the lights have not dimmed at all and that she is delusional. In this same way, gaslighting is a type of mental abuse where a person is manipulated into doubting their own memory, perception and ultimately their own sanity. It's a pervasive, insidious form of abuse akin to brainwashing where one person attempts to basically override and control the other person's reality.

This can range from simple denial of something (you remind the narcissist of something they did or said and the narcissist replies, That never happened! You're making it up!) to an elaborate staging of a situation designed to confuse and upset someone (you walk into your home after work and there is a party happening; you ask the narcissist what is going on and the narcissist responds, We had this party planned for a month! We talked about it all the time! What do you mean, you didn't know about it?) Gaslighting is designed to keep you off-balance and unsure so that the narcissist can control you - and everything else. Confused, frightened, doubtful people are much easier to manipulate and control than those who are very sure of themselves.

It should be noted here that being subjected to gaslighting is not an indication of weakness. Anybody can start to doubt themselves and their perceptions when they are subjected to this horrible mind game for months or even years on end, and anyone can be a victim of it. Gaslighting can also be more subtle and harder to define, which makes it even harder to detect - or prove. For example, you ask the narcissist why they are being cruel to you. Instead of actually addressing that, the narcissist says that you don't care about them. Instead of insisting that the narcissist answer this very reasonable question, you start defending yourself and then the point is lost. No one is talking about the narcissist's cruelty anymore. It has become all about you and what you are doing wrong. The narcissist insists that you don't care, listing a litany of complaints about how cruel and uncaring your behavior is. You become convinced the narcissist really believes this, so you begin overcompensating, trying to do things to prove you do care. The harder you try, the more the narcissist will deny you. The narcissist now sees that this can be used as a weapon to hurt you and manipulate you into doing what the narcissist wants you to do. The narcissist has won, and more importantly, the narcissist has avoided being taken to task over bad behavior.

Gaslighting is a way for narcissists to dodge responsibility for their actions, and to keep from ever having to answer for anything they've done. It's a way of saying "The problem isn't me, it's you." Just saying that isn't enough, however. This tactic can only work if they can actually convince you that it's true. They use gaslighting in order to do that. If gaslighting is successful, if the narcissist can convince the victim that the victim is not caring enough, or too sensitive, or crazy, or that the victim is actually the abuser, the narcissist never has to answer for anything ever again. This is the crux of what the narcissist is trying to do.

# HOW DOES GASLIGHTING AFFECT PEOPLE?

It takes a very strong person to completely withstand gaslighting, especially if they don't realize that's what is going on. As mentioned above, gaslighting is hard to detect and even harder to prove. The only way to fight gaslighting is to learn to recognize it for what it is. That is the only way you can stop it from damaging your self-image and your stability.

Remember: You are not the crazy one. You are not the wrong one. You are not the abuser, or the cruel one. You are not too sensitive. You are not uncaring or abusive just because you are a human being who makes mistakes and has feelings . Remind yourself that your perception has always been fine until now. Remind yourself that no one but the narcissist accuses you of these supposed perception problems. Remind yourself that no one but the narcissist accuses you of being a liar or an abuser or too sensitive... whatever the narcissist is trying to convince you of, remind yourself that no one but the narcissist sees it. Most importantly: don't lose sight of who you are. You know who you are. Don't let the narcissist take that away from you.

Narcissists such as Borderline, Histrionic, Narcissistic and Antisocial Personality-Disordered people are willing to sacrifice anybody for their own wants and needs. These wants and needs may fluctuate depending on what personality disorder the person has, but the end result is the same: they will sacrifice you in order to achieve these things. Narcissists want you to set yourself on fire to keep them warm. You say, "I'm dying! I'm burning to death!" and they say, "Well, I'm cold. Why don't you care that I'm cold? You selfish evil person, how can you be so heartless?" Your suffering is not important to them at all and in some cases, it's actually the icing on the cake. All narcissists - regardless of which personality disorder they are afflicted with - have a cruel, envious core in their personality. They are jealous, they are hurting and they want to destroy things they are jealous of, so there are times that being cruel brings them pleasure. You can sometimes even see it in their face.

This is because narcissists want you to prove that you love them. It makes them feel safe, true, but more than that, it makes them feel powerful. To that end, they will never stop trying to make you prove it. After you jump one hurdle, there are 15 more waiting. It never ends, and if you were to set yourself on fire to keep them warm, this would be more proof that you love them and more than that, it would be seen as how things are supposed to be. They are the special one and you are supposed to sacrifice for them without question. Over and over and over again. Borderline Personality disordered-people are especially bad about this. We often see the claim that Borderlines are not narcissists. Make no mistake about it: Borderline Personality Disordered-people are narcissists. They may have slightly different drives than Narcissistic Personality-Disordered people or Histrionics, for example, but they are still pathological narcissists. Their end goal is still having their own needs met regardless of the cost to other people. Anyone who has had a relationship with a Borderline Personality-disordered person can attest to that.

A narcissist who feels safe can be a dangerous narcissist; they may then feel there is no reason not to do terrible things because they are safe in the idea that you will never leave. Unfortunately, it is a trap that many people fall into, because when a non- personality disordered person is in a relationship, if our partner is not happy and they say it is because of something we are doing (or not doing) we tend to believe them. Why would they say it if it wasn't true? The sad truth is that narcissists need too much and they do claim things that aren't true all the time. They need more and want more than anyone can possibly give them and they are very angry that they aren't getting it. They are unreasonable, unrealistic and they don't understand give and take. They truly believe that they should be given everything, and any insinuation that they should give is perceived as blasphemy. Respect? Consideration? Compromise? These are not words narcissists understand as applying to other people. If they have to destroy your perception of yourself or your very reality in order to get what they want, they have no problem with that.

# ARE YOU BEING GASLIGHTED?

If you are not sure whether you are being gaslighted, here are a few things you can look for:

- ✓ if you are constantly second-guessing yourself
- ✓ if you have the sense that you used to be a very different person; someone who was happier and more confident
- ✓ if you have trouble making even simple decisions if you are always apologizing to the narcissist

- ✓ if you notice the narcissist making accusations or calling out behavior in you that no one has ever mentioned before
- ✓ if you feel confused or crazy and you don't know why

These are all signs that you may be being gaslighted. If you recognize any of these signs, please seek help or leave the relationship.

# HOW CAN YOU STOP GASLIGHTING?

There are 3 stages a person goes through when they are subjected to gaslighting. These are disbelief, defense and depression.

Disbelief is defined as when the gaslighting first happens and you just sort of dismiss it as a weird occurrence or something that was out of character but isolated. You don't recognize what is happening or if you do, you disregard it because you have feelings for the narcissist and don't want to acknowledge something they are doing wrong.

Defense is defined as the period of time when you are defending yourself against the accusations or manipulation. This stage can last a long time. As in our earlier example, let's say you ask the narcissist why they are being cruel to you and instead of actually addressing that, the narcissist says that you don't care about them. The narcissist might also say that you are imagining things, or that you are too sensitive or any number of things designed to take the focus off of their behavior and put it on yours. The end result is that the conversation becomes focused on you and how you are actually the problem. You defend, implore, remind, beseech, you do everything you can to prove these things are not true. This is where it becomes dangerous because though you are defending yourself, by doing so you have agreed that it is a problem worth talking about. The narcissist has manipulated you into agreeing it is all about you. The more you try to defend yourself, the crazier it will drive you and the more it convinces you that you really are the problem. If the narcissist would only see the truth, if you keep trying, the narcissist has to admit it, has to see it, has to believe it. Right? Wrong. They don't. And they never will, because they don't want to. This is probably the hardest thing for those who love a narcissist to understand and accept: they do not want to see you as a good person. They don't want to believe you and they are never going to. They want you to be just as horrible as they believe they themselves are, and they will do absolutely everything they can to prove that you are. It's a vicious cycle and the only way out is to stop participating in it.

Depression is when you have stopped defending yourself against the manipulation and just give up. You allow the narcissist to control your reality and suffer more every day, for no other reason than because a sick, miserable, disordered person wants you to be just as miserable, sick and disordered as they are.

This doesn't have to happen. You can learn to defeat gaslighting by not participating in it. Don't allow the narcissist to control the conversation; make them stick to the topic or stop the conversation. Don't allow the narcissist to deflect the conversation - and the blame - onto you; ignore all attempts to do so. Don't defend yourself against their accusations; you are validating the accusations by doing so.

Repeat: you are validating the accusations when you defend yourself against them. Ignore them. Don't continue the conversation when gaslighting is occurring. Calmly tell the narcissist that you know things did not occur that way and walk away. Gaslighting can only work if you let it work - and you don't have to anymore.

# Narcissists & Psychopaths: Surviving The Smear Campaign

What is a narcissistic smear campaign? If you've ever been unfortunate enough to be targeted by a malignant narcissist, then you know what it is, but for those of you who don't know, a smear campaign is when the narcissist attempts to cause you problems, turn other people against you and basically ruin your life with lies. They might tell other people you are crazy, that you are abusive, that you are a whore, that you are a drug user, a bad parent... whatever is the exact opposite of what you actually are. It's important to pay attention to exactly what lies they are telling, because within these lies is the reason they are doing it. Whatever they are trying to destroy about you is the thing they are jealous of.

For example: If they are telling everyone you are a bad parent, it is because you are seen by the narcissist as a better parent than they are. This cannot be permitted, so they attempt to destroy that perception of you. If they are saying you are abusive, this is because they know they are the abusive one. They are attempting to hide that by destroying the possibility that anyone could see you as the victim. They also would dearly love to be the victim but they know they are not. So they lie.

These lies are also projections; they are the narcissist taking the way that he feels or what he is and saying it is how you feel or what you are. If you want to understand the narcissist's language, reverse the pronouns. Whatever the narcissist is saying about you is what actually true about himself, or what he fears is true about himself. "You are abusive!" means, "I am abusive." "You are a bad parent!" means "I am a bad parent." "The kids love me more!" means, "The kids love you more." Statements they make about your feelings toward them can often have a double meaning. For instance, "You hate me!" means "I hate you!" and it also means "I hate myself." "You wish I was dead!" means "I wish you were dead!" and it also means, "I wish I was dead." Nobody escapes the narcissist's wrath, least of all himself. He's got plenty to go around.

# WHY DO MALIGNANT NARCISSISTS ENGAGE IN SMEAR CAMPAIGNS?

Narcissists engage in a smear campaign for two reasons. The first is that he is jealous of you for some reason. If you have a lot of friends or if people like you, if you have a very loving, supportive extended family, he is going to try to ruin that. No one likes him and no one loves him in his estimation, so if he can't have friends or family, nobody should have friends or family. Instead of realizing that he has no friends or family because of his own behavior and then working to be a better listener, to be more trustworthy and less incredibly selfish in order to gain more friendships, he simply decides that people dislike him because the world is unfair to him and therefore, he is going to right this egregious wrong perpetrated against him by deciding that it's unfair for anyone else to have something he cannot have. Why should the world only be unfair to him? Then he works to destroy these things for the other person. It's his idea of justice, in a very real sense.

For example, when asked why he would want to make people dislike a person he claimed to care about, a narcissist said, "Because you need to know what it's like not to be liked." The callousness and selfishness in that statement is really unbelievable. When it was pointed out to the narcissist that if he had to come up with lies in order to try to make people dislike someone, that proved the person didn't deserve it, he simply shrugged, "Why should I be the only one?" They just want to spread the misery, even to the people who love them. Especially to the people who love them. Remember, the narcissist views himself as so broken and terrible that the very fact a person could love him must mean something is very wrong with that person. Because of this, he feels the people who love him must be broken and terrible, too, and they deserve abuse and punishment.

This is the second reason they engage in smear campaigns. It is quite literally to make you miserable. They want you to be unhappy because they are unhappy. In the end, it's really no deeper or more complicated than that. The world is unfair to them, so they will be unfair to you. It's very important to realize that to them, this is not unfair. It's justice. This is why they often never stop unless they are forced to stop.

They really cannot see that their misery is all their own fault. No one likes people who are cruel, who are liars, who are phonies, who are instigators, who are childish and petty and vindictive and abusive. The malignant narcissist is all of these things but he cannot understand the way that other people see him. He really believes he deserves everything he wants and that the world is against him. Maybe it is, but not unfairly. If the world is against him, it's because people universally dislike someone who is selfish, cruel and hateful who will stop at nothing to hurt or destroy other people. This is one reason it is so hard to get a narcissist to see what he is doing wrong.

He doesn't think he IS wrong. As far as he is concerned, you are wrong for daring to have more people who love you than he does and you deserve to have that taken from you because you flaunted it in his face. You might say, "But I didn't!" Oh, but you did. Your life, your very existence is flaunting it in his face and he will not rest until you are taken off that pedestal and brought back down to reality. Sound ridiculous? Not to the narcissist. To the narcissist, it is very real and he lives it every day. This is what you are up against: a obsessive mind enraged with jealousy who takes your very existence as a personal attack and a personal insult.

# HOW DO YOU COUNTERACT A SMEAR CAMPAIGN?

I wish I could tell you that you don't have to, that people will not believe the narcissist's lies but unfortunately, this is just not the truth. Some people will. And it often seems that the bigger the lies are, the more people believe it. Maybe they just can't believe somebody would make that up so it must be true. This can also work the opposite way as well. Take the situation of the physically abusive narcissist. Every time he hits his wife, she tries to call the police. The narcissist then begins punching himself in the face and says, "Go ahead and call them. I have marks on me and you don't. We'll see who goes to jail, me or you." The wife then hangs up the phone. She feels the police will not believe a grown man hit himself like that, and she will be arrested instead. Sadly, she's probably right. Who would believe that? Who even does that? It sounds completely, totally absurd, a story no one would ever believe. The narcissist knows that. He uses that. When we are tempted to believe these behaviors are out of the narcissist's control or something they cannot help, we should remember the calculated planning involved in that story. That is a true story. Narcissists know exactly what they are doing. They are doing it on purpose, in a very calculated way so that they can continue to get away with the horrible things they do. The physically abusive narcissist did not want to go to jail. He wanted to keep beating on his wife and he would have been perfectly happy to let her go to jail for something she did not do in order to save himself. If it comes down to a choice between you and the narcissist – or anybody and the narcissist - the narcissist is going to choose himself every time.

The best you can do is ignore a smear campaign. This doesn't sound like much and it isn't, but unless you can prove that it is the narcissist saying these things and that the things being said are not true, there is nothing you can do except make sure you never appear to be what he says you are. If you can prove it, do so! Go to a judge or the police or whoever there is to go to where you live and show them. Take whatever legal or civil action you can and pursue it as far as you have to. Remember: you are dealing with pathological obsession and jealousy here; it probably will not just go away. Stay away from the narcissist. Have No Contact with them. If you have to have contact, be sure to always keep control of yourself. Write down dates, keep a journal of what was said, record the conversations if you can - video is even better - and keep it all. Keep a journal of the things the narcissist is saying about you to others, as well. If he says it on social media or in text messages, or if other people text you or private message you about it, take screen shots. Keep a record of what he is doing. It is your only proof and the only way to fight.

# How to Stop Reacting & Break The Drama Cycle of Borderlines, Narcissists & Psychopaths

How do you stop reacting to the provocations of borderlines, histrionics, narcissists and psychopaths? Before we can understand how to break the cycle, we must first understand why narcissists such as histrionics, borderlines, narcissistic personality disordered people and psychopaths try to provoke others in the first place. There are a few reasons.

## THE WHY

They are bored. That sounds like a lame reason but these types of people don't experience boredom the way the rest of us do. Boredom is experienced by them as incredibly oppressive, even crushing or scary and they will do anything to escape it. If that means they have to provoke a fight with you, they will do so with no problem. It is more important that they feel better than it is to respect or care about your feelings. That is of course, the main theme when dealing with narcissists in general. When it comes down to choosing between you and themselves, they will always choose themselves. Attached to this reason is the fact that many of these types of people have impulse control problems and a complete lack of respect for others, which leads to whatever they think just coming out of their mouths. This leads to constant arguments and problems with other people.

They are hypersensitive to real or imagined criticism, so many times they don't actually feel they are provoking the incident. They feel that you have done something to them and they are defending themselves. This leads to circular arguments that consist of a "No I didn't/yes you did" type of dynamic where the bewildered partner spends hours trying to explain to the narcissist that the narcissist has misunderstood or is mistaken. Nothing can ever be solved because they insist that you have "bad intentions" or dastardly motives and you cannot prove that you didn't. Who could? There is no reasoning with this. What they feel is how it is. They feel you had a nasty motive, so it becomes a fact that you did and you will be punished for that. It doesn't matter how much proof there is to the contrary. It will be ignored or twisted against you because the truth is, they don't want to believe you anyway. These people fit the facts to their feelings, rather than their feelings to the facts. They want to be the victim because it's the only way they can escape the feeling that they are so horrible. If a person is a victim, they cannot also be the bad guy. This is also why they will never admit that they are abusing the other person. If they admit the other person is a victim, then it means the narcissist is the bad guy. That is intolerable for them. So they automatically interpret everything as something bad against them, therefore they are always the victim and never the bad guy.

Narcissists like provoking the emotions of others. They believe it means others care, in one way or another. They truly do not care whether they are given negative attention or positive, as long as they are getting it. If they cannot be the best, they will be the worst. If they cannot make you love them (which they think they cannot do, regardless of how much you tell them you DO love them), then they will make you hate them. At least then, they are still important. They matter. You care. You are reacting. You are feeding their ego, which demands itself to be recognized. Narcissists are psychic vampires so this is very, very important to them and however far they have to take it to get to this, that is how far it will go.

They are sick, miserable disordered people who need to lash out. This is perhaps the saddest and most awful of all reasons that narcissists provoke others. They hate you, they hate themselves, they hate everything and they just can't hold it in anymore. The world is not fair. They were given a disorder that they did not ask for, they are miserable and unhappy and afraid and angry and it's not fair that everyone else gets to be happy when they don't. So they actively try to ruin things for others. It makes them feel better. Maybe they are not happy, but now neither is anybody else. This makes them feel powerful and less vulnerable. It's like a drug for them. They are literally addicted to your pain. It's the only thing that makes them feel better.

# THE HOW

So how do you stop reacting to this constant onslaught of emotional extortion, provocation, hysteria and blows below the belt? Well, you just stop. That's it. It's harder than it sounds, but easier than you think. You see, part of the reason that people react the way they do in situations is because it is what we are used to doing, and especially in high-emotion or dramatic situations (as there always are with these types of people), your body starts to think this is how it is supposed to function all the time. However, the good news is that the body was trained into that and it can be trained out of it the same way. It's about making different choices. That is what you have to focus on here: your choices. You cannot control your narcissistic loved one or coworker. They can't even control themselves. You can only control yourself and that is what you have to do. Just stop reacting.

It goes in steps. First, you control the behavior. If your reaction is to start yelling, stop yelling. If your reaction is to start crying, stop crying. If your reaction is to call names or insult the narcissist back, stop doing that. You will feel the reaction in you, and it will want to come out. Your body is trying to do what it has always been doing. But you are in control - unlike the narcissist. The narcissist does not control your reactions. You do. Take a deep breath and tell yourself, "I am not going to react. That is what the narcissist wants and I am not going to give it to them." This really does work. Ignore the provocation by not responding at all if you can and if you can't, such as you are having a necessary communication with the narcissist, simply assert your point or answer the question and nothing else. Don't acknowledge the insult or the guilt trip. Just let it go. If you cannot stop yourself from having a reaction, leave the room. They are trying to control and manipulate your feelings, but it can only work if you let it work. They have no power that you did not give them. You can take the power back and reclaim control over your life, your mind and your emotions. This is how you start.

After you have consistently stopped reacting, you will notice the narcissist ramps up the abuse and the provocation, trying harder to upset you and get you to react. Just keep ignoring it. After you've done this for a length of time, you will notice that your body and mind no longer respond the way they used to. You won't feel the reaction anymore. This is where you want to be. If you crack occasionally, don't beat yourself up. These people are masters at manipulation. The important thing is to react less and less until you don't react at all. And remember: it does not mean you don't care. It means that you are asserting control over your own life, your own mind and your own emotions the way that healthy people are supposed to do. This is not wrong for you to do, it's right and it has nothing to do with how much you care about the narcissist. For once, it's not about them. It's about you.

# How to Get Rid of The Narcissists or Psychopath in Your Life

Living with a borderline personality, a pathological narcissist or their "end-stage" counterpart, the psychopath is one of the most difficult and frankly horrible things a person is likely to do in their lifetime. These people are malignant narcissists; they are abusive, manipulative, destructive and corrosive, endeavoring to cause as much damage to someone as they possibly can before moving on. Some may never move on if they are not emphatically convinced to do so. So how do you get rid of them? The key lies in understanding what drives the borderline, the narcissist and the psychopath to fixate on someone in the first place.

## THE WHY

The first thing to understand is that even though the underlying trauma that created the malignant narcissist might be very complex, the malignant narcissists themselves are not. These are simple personalities, and very childlike in their desires and needs. They are driven by envy and boredom, in that order. That's it.

If we were to look at these personalities as the sort of adult equivalent of a two year old that is taking another child's toy in order to make that child cry, we see a very good metaphor for how they work. And how do you stop this behavior in children? You stop encouraging it. This is what you must do with the adult malignant narcissist in your life: stop encouraging the behavior. If the two year old in our analogy can no longer provoke the emotional response he is looking for, or if the object of envy (the toy) is gone, he will stop his behavior in very short order and move on to something else. The same is true with malignant narcissists. They seek to control others through provoking emotional responses, and through destroying things they envy. If you simply stop responding, you take their control away. This is extremely important, so it bears repeating: If you stop responding, you take their control away.

How do you do that? The answer lies in two words.

# BE BORING.

It sounds simple, and it really is. Malignant narcissists such as the borderline, the pathological narcissist and the psychopath crave upheaval, emotional fireworks, drama and excitement. They attack and abuse out of boredom and envy. Don't give them anything to envy and stop responding to their attacks.

The latter in particular can be very difficult to do; these people have honed their attacks and abuse to be very, very effective. It cuts their loved ones to the quick, like an arrow in the gut. They are masters at inspiring rage or extreme anxiety in other people with just a few short phrases, and some can do it without even saying a word. They are counting on this. This reaction is exactly what they want, so don't give it to them. Be boring. Be beige. Envision a grey rock in your mind. How would a grey rock respond to the malignant narcissist's abuse? A-ha! That's a trick question, because it wouldn't. It would sit there, inflexible and serene. In a word, boring. Be a grey rock, or a blank white wall. Ignore threats, hysteria, insults or whatever else is said. They're just words anyway. Respond when you must but never in an emotional way:

Attack that must be responded to: "Why did you spend $50 out of the account?! You're so irresponsible/stupid/careless/selfish/etc.!"

Non-emotional response: "I had to buy groceries."

Attack that must be responded to: "When are you ever going to let me see my kids after/now that we are divorced?? You just want to take them from me and turn them against me! You're a horrible mother/father!"

Non-emotional response: "You can see our kids [whenever s/he is supposed to, according to the custody agreement]."

That's it. In a very controlled voice, with no emotion at all. Don't defend yourself, don't apologize, don't give excuses, don't insult in response. Simply answer the question and leave it at that. The malignant narcissist will undoubtedly continue for a little while in this vein to attempt to provoke a response out of you, stepping up the insults and using things he knows will hurt or anger you. Don't give in. Only respond if you must (such as when asked a valid question) and then only in a polite and disinterested way; do not allow emotions to become a part of the conversation in any way. Don't argue. (This does not mean give in to everything the malignant narcissist wants or says; by all means, stick to your guns and state your side if you really have to – but don't argue. It's a pretty safe bet that he does not know how to handle a person who does not become enraged or hurt by his "style" of arguing, so if you absolutely must respond, be that person.) Remember: this has always been a two-way street, even if it didn't seem to be, with the malignant narcissist taking and you giving. By controlling your own emotions, you are able to take control away from the malignant narcissistic personality in your life.

Envy is a little trickier. It has more to do with who they are as a person. Malignant narcissists such as borderlines, pathological narcissists and psychopaths envy other people many things, because inside they know that they are not truly a "real person." If somebody has a talent or a good quality, the malignant narcissist endeavors to take these things away from that somebody. They will do whatever they can to destroy or disrupt it - and they delight in doing so. The trick here is to hide it from them so they cannot do that. They are also simple creatures, and they are attracted to anything shiny and pretty. Unfortunately with the malignant narcissist, "attraction" means "envy," which means "attempts to destroy."

How do you stop giving them things to envy? Be boring! Now, you might say, "But he already says I'm boring/lame/not exciting... How can this work for me?" Simple: because he lies. If that were really true, he would have already moved on. He is simply trying to destroy your confidence and crush your good qualities. He is also projecting on to you what he thinks and/or fears about himself. Don't listen to him. The bottom line with any malignant narcissistic personality - be they borderline, pathological narcissist or psychopath - is this: he is the uncontested king of needing constant stimulation; if he stays with you, you are not boring.

No matter what he says, there is something, some spark about you that caught his attention in the first place and which keeps him hanging on. So stop doing all the things you did that attracted the malignant narcissist in the first place. Don't be funny. Don't be outgoing. Don't be passionate. Don't be emotional. Don't be smart, pretty, charismatic or exciting and above all: don't argue. Just be a grey rock. This of all things will cause him to lose interest the fastest. Malignant narcissistic personalities do not experience boredom in the same way normal people do. It is experienced by them as incredibly oppressive, even terrifying in some ways and must be avoided at all costs. So pile on the boredom and watch what happens.

# IS THIS FAIR?

In a word, no. It's not. No one should have to hide all of their good qualities and dramatically change their personality to become a grey rock just to get away from another person. However, since you're reading this you've probably already figured out that the malignant narcissist is not interested in fairness - at all. He's interested in controlling other people and using them for his own personal entertainment and validation by needlessly upsetting, torturing and abusing them. That's it. He doesn't care about other people's feelings at all, except to the extent that he can use them to hurt or dominate someone else. He's not a real person and he will never become one.

If you are trying to do anything with a malignant narcissist based on some idea of fairness, you are going to be very, very disappointed and probably also very, very sorry. Understand that the situation is not fair to you, has never been fair to you, will never be fair to you and then work with it. It's the only way it can be successful. Otherwise, you will find yourself locked in a power struggle with the malignant narcissist until the end of time, with him using that sense of equality against you nonstop. He will use it to manipulate your sense of fairness into excusing his terrible behavior by calling you unfair, and he will use it as a weapon because he knows it hurts you, such as being deliberately unfair and cruel so he can watch the pain it causes you. It's all unfair, but this is where we find ourselves. It's hard especially after being mistreated - but let it go. It's more important to get the malignant narcissist out of your life before they can do any more damage.

# Conclusion

I put this together because everything I've read or heard tries to get people to empathize with the narcissist and validate them and all of these things. While I understand why they tell people to do it, I do not see the use of it in a real-life situation. It does not make anything better. In many ways, it can make things worse, and often people report that eventually, the validation and empathy they attempted to give the narcissist was twisted and used as another way to manipulate or punish them, or that it was only effective for a very short time. Too frequently, the advice we see revolves around the non-personality-disordered person rearranging or learning new ways to do, say and think everything so as not to upset the narcissist and pacify them to keep the peace. This is unfair and unrealistic. It also means that the entire family situation still has to revolve around the narcissist, which is exactly what the narcissist wants. It can actually reinforce their narcissism. Much of the advice commonly given also refuses to directly address the conscious cruelty and large scale manipulation that most of these people engage in. It tries too hard to present them as victims. They certainly are victims, but to simply ignore the fact that narcissists are doing many of these terrible things on purpose is dangerous and it's counterproductive. That may be why the "textbook advice" that we usually get regarding how to deal with narcissists often does not work in a real-life situation with a real-life narcissist. People's homes are not psychiatric hospitals or group therapy sessions, and most people are not doctors. I feel there is a real need to give common-sense, practical information, and teach common-sense, practical techniques for dealing with personality-disordered people.

www.ingramcontent.com/pod-product-compliance
Lightning Source LLC
Chambersburg PA
CBHW031256250726
48655CB00005B/2245